THE MARKETING MACHINE®
FOR
PROFESSIONAL SERVICES

Endless quality referrals for lawyers,
accountants, consultants and more

Joseph A. Krueger
&
Virginia S. Nicols

Dentrovisi, Inc.

Irvine, California

Copyright © 2019 by **Joseph A. Krueger and Virginia S. Nicols**

All rights reserved. No part of this publication may be reproduced, distributed or transmitted in any form or by any means, without prior written permission.

Dentrovisi, Incorporated
4790 Irvine Blvd., Suite 105
Irvine, CA 92620

The Marketing Machine® for Professional Services -- Joseph A. Krueger and Virginia S. Nicols -- 1st ed.
ISBN: 978-1-7200582-0-5

Dedication

Three mentors are largely "to blame" for my consulting career:

Pete Shugart, Industrial Direct Mail Consultant – Pete insisted that I had a natural instinct for Direct Response Advertising and began referring clients before I even knew what I was getting into.

Dick Hammond, Mailing List Broker – Dick taught me about the list, the single most important factor in getting breakthrough response to Direct Marketing campaigns.

Hank Burnett, Copywriter and Creative Director – Hank taught me that great advertising copy comes easily once you have the strategy right . . . not before!

Joe Krueger

Disclaimer

The purpose of this book is to educate, and not to provide you with any legal, accounting, or other form of business advice. As the authors and publisher, Dentrovisi, Incorporated dba The Marketing Machine® does not warrant that the information contained in this report is fully complete and we shall not be responsible for any errors, omissions, or contradictory information. You as reader bear the responsibility to verify the contents. We urge you to be especially diligent in this because the business landscape in which we are all working is changing rapidly.

Your success with using the techniques and ideas in the book is not guaranteed. Each individual's success depends on his/her dedication, motivation, and background. As with any business endeavor, there is an inherent risk of loss of capital; you assume full responsibility for how you use these materials and information.

The Marketing Machine® is a federally registered trademark of Joseph A. Krueger and Dentrovisi Incorporated (licensee).

Contents

PREFACE i

INTRODUCTION xi

1 - Understanding the Business You Are Really In 1

    Okay, let's talk about sales. Yes, your sales. 5

    Marketing is more than sponsorships and trinkets. 7

    You do have to understand what's holding you back 8

    The answer? Let others do the pre-selling for you. 11

    Hold This Thought: 12

2 – Aren't My Credentials and Degrees My Real Marketing? 15

    Unfortunately, most professionals are behind the times. 15

    Fast forward to today's hyper speed marketplace. 17

    Selling professional services is "pulling" as opposed to "pushing." 20

The disciplined sales process requires a number of marketing tools. 20

Hold This Thought: 24

3 - Referrals May Be The Best Source of Clients . . . But Are They Always? 25

A referral system starts with your network . . . your "sphere of influence." 27

Personal contacts are not your best referral source over the long haul. 28

The best referrals will start to come from people who don't know you. 29

What role does social media play in your prospecting? 32

Hold This Thought: 34

4 - How Do I Know Which Referrals Will Be Profitable? 35

Putting a dollar value on your average client..35

Using the LTCV formula.....................36

Build a "profile" of the clients on List 1. 37

Build referral source profiles for lists 2 and 3...42

Hold This Thought: 46

5 - Selling Professional Services is a Two Phase Process 47

   The successful professional masters the art of "reverse selling." 48

   Another name for this process is "attraction marketing." 50

   Authority marketing attracts qualified inquiries. 51

   How do you achieve "authority" status? 52

   Hold This Thought: 54

6- Shaping your Practice with a Good Marketing Plan 55

   Your plan matches client needs with your firm's strengths. 59

   The Plan's flaws will be revealed early on. 60

   What strategies will you be testing? ... 61

   Don't overlook classic marketing tools and tactics. 62

   Definitely incorporate electronic or online media. 63

No matter the medium, professional services marketing requires discipline. 65

Hold This Thought: 70

7 - The Professional's Sales Process and The Role of Each Stage 71

Hold your fire until you see the whites of their eyes. 71

Each step in the sales sequence "sells" only the next step. 81

Hold This Thought: 84

8 --Building Your Brand and Selling into "The Long Game" 85

Back to the drawing board for the Unique Value Proposition 88

Hold This Thought: 94

9 - Using Direct Mail to Generate Leads and Stimulate Referrals 95

The bottom line: You don't care about the cost of the mailing. 101

"Well, let's try some direct mail to see if it works." 106

Hold This Thought: 112

10 - Feeding Your Referral Engine 115

Why is pro bono work important and how do you make it win-win? 118

What about attending conventions? 120

With so many potential marketing activities, where should I begin? 123

Hold This Thought: 126

11 - Your Website is the Hub of Your Marketing Plan. 127

Hold This Thought: 140

12 - The Role of Publishing in Establishing Your "Authority" 141

Rest easy. Help is everywhere for you. 142

Hold This Thought: 147

Appendices 149

1 - The Marketing Machine® for Professional Services – THE WORKBOOK 151

2-Conferences and Conventions: Seven Questions to Ask Before You Invest in Your Next One 153

Introduction – The Conference Investment...................................... 154

Question One – Have You Picked The Right Show?........................... 156

Question Two – Have You Set Specific Goals For This Show? 159

Question Three – Who Do You Want To Connect With?.......................... 161

Question Four – Do You Have A Cheat Sheet For Each Session? 164

Question Five – Are You Primed For Networking? 166

Question Six – What's Your Plan For Following Up?................................ 169

Question Seven – How Do You Measure Value? 172

Final Thoughts 173

3-The Direct Mail Process 175

4-Write your book! 177

5- *Business Survival Project*: a Lead Generation Program uniquely suited for professional services firms 179

Some Final Words and a Couple of Offers from the Authors...................................183

PREFACE

Why another book on sales and marketing? Hasn't everything that can be said about advertising, marketing and sales already been said, re-said, regurgitated and published in virtually every form possible?

Whether the answer is "yes" or not, some people still haven't gotten the message. Why not?

That's not an easy question to answer but a little history will give you an idea of why we are addressing it here.

I'll keep this short and then give you a three point answer.

OUR HISTORY MADE IT POSSIBLE.

I (Joe) got into the marketing world pretty much by accident. Having started off my professional life as an electronics engineer-turned counterspy and industrial security executive, I came into the field with an odd set of expectations. Virginia, trained as an educator-turned-Financial-Planner, was a marketer by default, being responsible for building the client base for her firm.

We began specializing in lead generation programs for major corporations, including financial giants like American Express, Charles Schwab, Bank One, Wells Fargo and scores of others. What we learned about the business of generating inquiries for products and services would set new standards for the creation and strategic use of direct mail by corporate America.

Three decades later, happily laden with accolades, awards and a history of nearly $5 Billion in sales for national and international clients, Virginia and I decided to change focus. For the past few years we have been working with professional services providers, smaller, socially responsible businesses and environmentally friendly organizations that couldn't afford major marketing agencies.

We expect this book to be criticized for lumping all professional services together and we accept the criticism. But we're starting this way because we've discovered some consistent themes that seem to apply in all these businesses.

Maybe that's because professionals are, by definition, a breed apart!

In any case, we will soon hit the press with the rest of the series: The Marketing Machine® for Accountants, the Marketing Machine® for Attorneys and The Marketing Machine ® for Financial Advisors, etc. Each will address specific ways these professionals can aggressively promote their services, but always with dignity and respect for their prospects and their competitors.

THESE PROBLEMS MAKE IT NECESSARY.

Our objective in writing this book is to address the three most important points in the professional's marketing activities that are all too often neglected in whole or in part:

- <u>First</u> - Most marketing books directed to professional services offer a single recommended solution to their lead generation needs. The recommendation is usually more about the author's experience and biases than about the reader's personal needs and actual capabilities.

  We recommend that a system of business development be built around the particular skills of the principals, the characteristics of their marketplace and their positioning vis-à-vis the competition. Even though it's a "system," every system will be different.

- <u>Second</u> - While no one denies the importance of referrals to a professional service, most fail to address the need for controls on the nature, quantity and quality of referrals. The truth is that unsolicited referrals can be inappropriate for the firm's skillset, its size or current needs. Without the controls of disciplined management they can be disruptive to the firm and ultimately be proven unprofitable and even disastrous.

- <u>Third</u> - Perhaps the single most important message we have for members of the professional services – and in particular the small office "solopreneurs" – is to avoid the tendency toward "roller coaster marketing." We all love the work we do for clients. We want to give our all on their behalf. In so doing, though, when we're flush with business we sell ourselves short! We neglect marketing for our most important long-term client . . . ourselves.

We hope you will find our challenges to these three points worthy of your purchase and that you'll look forward to our future works, particularly when we focus directly on your specialty.

Joseph Krueger & Virginia Nicols

About the **Business Marketing Series**

When we sat down to write *The Marketing Machine® for Professional Services* we envisioned it as a general guide to businesses serving the Small-to-Medium-sized Business (SMB) community. The book features advertising, marketing and sales strategies and techniques that we have employed over the years with considerable success – and ROI --for major as well as boutique organizations.

In large part, those successes, and the examples in the book, come from the world of Direct Marketing.

As we were writing, it became clear that we had more information and examples to share that **applied to specific professions or industries**. We were frustrated that we couldn't include them all!

Thus the first book became the impetus for an entire series. As of this 2019 update, we now have three basic volumes, accompanied in each case with a workbook. (Reading is one way to learn. Writing adds a whole other perspective!)

The
Business Marketing Series
from
The Marketing Machine®

Each book in the series is written for the small business professional. The companion workbook follows the same flow, breaking it up into questions so that you can easily customize the content for your own business.

We've created **specific books and workbooks for Accountants and Attorneys** who work with small business clients.

While each book focuses on a specific profession or industry, there are many similarities between basic concepts and recommendations. As a result, you may see some selective and purposeful duplication of material from one book to another. After all, marketing and sales basics are precisely that – basics that apply across the board.

But in each volume, **many of our personal comments, our cautions and even whole discussions of "marketing psychology" come from experience** we've had with your specific profession.

We trust you will recognize those specifics. And we hope you'll be able to turn them to personal advantage as you build your own successful business.

INTRODUCTION

This is a book about marketing your professional practice. What can you expect from it?

First, be warned that it is not an all-encompassing book on marketing and selling. We struggled with the temptation to create a more thorough work, but came to the conclusion that too much detail for too wide an audience would run the risk of misleading some readers.

Besides, the reality today is that thick volumes simply don't get read by busy people. And our target audience is mostly working professionals who can benefit by narrowing their marketing efforts to fit their skillset.

I trust you fit that definition!

First, we will explore a number of media that can play a role in promoting your firm and your services. This overview will make you feel a lot more comfortable about marketing options in general. You will notice that we do not dwell on social media, and that's on purpose. We find that the popularity of various social media fluctuates and how to use the different platforms changes regularly. Our goal is to create a **systematic** marketing program, so we tend to focus on media that can be controlled.

Second, as you learn more about each of the options, you'll find it easier to **pick just the ones that make sense for you.** We'll simplify things even more by steering you **away** from some of them!

Third, by the time you're through, you'll have a good idea of how to **get started on your customized plan.**

Your plan has to be customized, because marketing a professional practice just isn't the same as marketing a company that sells a product or, for that matter, a service. And YOUR practice is a reflection of you as well as of your specialty, which makes it even more distinctive.

(To make it even easier, we've published a companion WORKBOOK to accompany this volume. Watch for more about it in the Appendix.)

Let's look into that a bit more deeply.

WHAT SETS THE PROFESSIONAL PRACTICE APART?

Your professional practice is different from a company that sells a product. Three things that make it different:

You're selling your talents, knowledge and experience as the solution to a problem, very often **a unique problem**. (Certainly, clients believe their problems are unique!) A one-size-fits-all solution (product) won't do, and can't effectively be advertised.

Because of the **personal nature of the relationship**, the practice takes on a big risk -- coming up with a customized solution that fits the client perfectly. And to lessen the risk, you need clients who fit your skills.

The **value of the solution** often needs to be defined – and it's best when you help a client define it up front. This allows you to charge what you need to charge!

All this "uniqueness" sounds pretty hard to make a plan around, I know. But there is a common thread that runs through all marketing for professional services, and that's what this book is all about.

All businesses benefit from referrals. Professionals can't survive without them. Moreover,

NO PROFESSIONAL PRACTICE CAN PROSPER WITHOUT A CONTINUOUS FLOW OF LEGITIMATE REFERRALS.

Why is it so hard to get that flow going? Here are a couple of thoughts about that, based on many years' experience.

The common wisdom is that referrals are free.

Nothing could be further from the truth!

Certainly, the person making a legitimate referral does not normally anticipate payment. On the other hand, if you expect friends, associates and clients to offer legitimate referrals then you have to educate them!

More than that, you have to educate each referral source – friend, associate or client – differently. All that educating certainly isn't free.

Another common assumption is that if people know you well, they are in a position to give you great referrals.

And again, this "wisdom" is flawed. Genuine respect or enthusiasm for you as a person helps, but if your referral sources don't understand what it is you really do, generally how much you charge and which of their friends or associates is likely to be the "right fit" for your services, they are likely to send you absolutely the WRONG referrals!

Remember the comment above about our "steering you away from some marketing methods?" Well, here's a piece of advice to start with:

THE WRONG REFERRALS COST YOU MORE THAN MONEY.

Referrals to the wrong people put you in a difficult, even embarrassing position. They waste your time. They tie up your emotions. They cost you money.

And because you can't serve them well, they can poison the well for future business.

Our goal with this book is to help you build a healthy referral "system" based on a solid understanding of your own strengths, the kinds of problems you solve and the kinds of clients you welcome.

A couple of afterthoughts . . .

I know of no other business category where "chemistry" is more important than for professionals. Clients are buying you perhaps even more than what you're selling. Getting to know, like and trust you is key to that chemistry you want to be present as you embark on this new relationship.

Building a business so dependent on people and knowledge is a balancing act. If you wake up one morning and find 70% of your base revenues coming from one client, your alarm bells should be going off along with the alarm clock.

Unbalanced growth can strain your finances as well as your staffing . . . and your reputation. Some choices are likely on your horizon!

1 - Understanding the Business You Are Really In

You are really in the business of marketing and sales.

Great marketing reduces reliance on sales techniques.

What's holding you back?

Let's get this book off to the right start with a mantra. Find a full length mirror. Plant yourself in front of it and repeat after me . . .

"I am in the marketing and sales business. I am the chief 'rainmaker' for my firm which is supported by sales."

Write this down and start off each day by standing in front of the mirror and repeating it ten times and don't waiver from this routine until you can honestly say that you truly believe it!

Silly? Absolutely! And it always embarrasses me to even suggest it to an accomplished professional like you. But I really need to make a point here.

(And don't think I'll be done with this rant soon! I'll be coming back to it periodically throughout the book because it's something I've been bumping up against for over four decades!)

Professionals are out there looking for a magic bullet to generate paying clients without having to do any selling.

There is no magic bullet. But there is magic to be found in marketing.

The better job you do in crafting your marketing, the more prepared the prospects that it attracts will be. The more prepared they are, the more prepared they will be to buy and the less "selling" you will need to do.

Let's take this a step further since this book is really about attracting referrals.

Your marketing efforts . . .

- **Identify** people or companies who are either most likely to need your services or are likely to work with people or companies they can refer to you.
- **Educate** these potential clients or referral candidates about the kind of referral to make.

Our role here is **not to send** you qualified clients, but to counsel you on the most effective **ways to attract** the right people and prepare them to think like clients.

Together, we are in the business of designing an ongoing process that generates inquiries in the form of "sales leads" and that makes it easy and logical for you to respond with what would otherwise be known as a sales process or sales funnel, or sometimes as the sales sequence.

The multi-step process ultimately concludes with a sales presentation.

But, before we explore the mechanics of the professional sales process, we must discuss another potentially uncomfortable reality.

This is the ever-present contempt that some sophisticated professional business owners have for the "sales" activity. They want new clients, but not at the expense of their dignity.

(If you don't fall into this category, please just ignore my thoughtless criticisms of your colleagues or your competitors.)

So strong is the aversion to selling in much of the professional world that the principals are willing to leave hundreds of thousands – even millions – of dollars on the table to avoid having to make a sales pitch to a prospective client.

We find this to be counterproductive and more than a little baffling. But then we really love sales.

I once sold premium cookware, door-to-door. I loved it. I saw myself as a Food Preparation Consultant, which had a professional ring to it. Virginia was a successful financial planner early in her career and was trained by a classic foot-in-the-door salesman. (She quickly found better ways to find clients than going door-to-door.) The point is, we've had some practice! As you read through this book you will notice, though, that our career success has revolved around communications . . . most of it in the form of written communications.

OKAY, LET'S TALK ABOUT SALES. YES, YOUR SALES.

Sales are the real business that you are in. If you don't make sales you don't have revenue. If you don't have revenue, you're not in business. Period.

Now I don't want to pick on anybody in particular and get accused of "selectively pontificating" so let's do this alphabetically and start with accountants and attorneys. In the interests of inclusion, we'll pick on business advisers and consultants in general before we throw in some additional professions for good measure.

The basic point I want to get across is that as a professional you have some unique challenges when it comes to promoting your services.

Here's one reality . . .

Whether you agree that the glut of lawyers is abating, there are still more of them in the U.S. than the market will bear. If you're an attorney, and you want a successful practice, you'd better have a unique niche and/or get famous real quick. Even a modest command of the written word would be a big differentiating benefit!

Now it used to be that doctors, lawyers, dentists and others were prevented by their associations from overtly and blatantly advertising their "professional" services.

Those days are long gone!

Annual advertising revenue for the legal profession has now crossed the $1 billion mark. And, while that still seems only barely significant compared to the $6 billion being spent by the pharmaceutical world (for example), professionals have to be clever in the way they advertise so as not to lose credibility.

Clever, yes, but . . .

MARKETING IS MORE THAN SPONSORSHIPS AND TRINKETS.

Accountants and architects aren't at the forefront of the spending frenzy, but they too find they have to venture into the unfamiliar world of marketing.

Accountants have some distinctive challenges. Many aren't particularly gregarious by nature and the term "bean counter" is an unfortunate but often-used term. Many of the marketing strategies they could be using are alien to them. For example, they find it tough to move into a position of being a financial consultant to their clients – the strategy that many competitors are mastering in order to grow.

And because marketing is foreign to many of these professionals, they often don't differentiate between "strategy" and "tactics."

This makes them sitting ducks for the specialty ad salespeople and they end up spending hard-earned dollars on cups, pens and notepads. And, occasionally, entire advertising programs that don't deliver results.

There are solutions to this!

You don't need aggressive advertising to survive.

YOU DO HAVE TO UNDERSTAND WHAT'S HOLDING YOU BACK.

Despite the advertising breakthrough in the professional world, there is still a tendency among conservative professionals to want to cling to their dignity. Why do you suppose these firms feel the need to keep their marketing, advertising and sales low key? Is it really just a carryover from their more restrictive history?

I'm sure history is at least a factor for some. But there is far more at play here.

Let's take a look at three of the factors holding professionals back from being smarter marketers. Hopefully we'll get to all the core issues before the book ends.

First is the issue of credentials. Most professionals have acquired degrees and citations that are indicative of their extensive and specialized education. Taken by themselves, credentials – which are shared by their competitors – often get lost in the highly competitive, consumer-driven world. (We'll deal with this in more detail in the next chapter.)

Second is the challenge of creating advertising that appeals to the particular client that the professional practice is specialized in serving. These specific prospective clients (or patients) are usually scattered amongst the population making it difficult and costly to even identify them, much less engage in a meaningful dialog. And while social media promised small and locally-situated businesses a cost-effective way to level the playing field, its effectiveness has been steadily eroded by increasing competition for the ads from larger corporations.

<u>Third</u> and most important is psychological positioning. Selling yourself is not the same as selling a product. And separating yourself from the service you offer is tricky. Finally, for you as a highly-educated, accomplished professional, selling your own services puts you in the position of appearing superior -- hardly a good approach for establishing rapport and building a good working relationship!

So you are naturally reluctant to consider promotions. Your reluctance is actually more than just psychological. Whether you're in the business of healthcare, financial counseling or legal services, you aren't able to guarantee an outcome for your clients or patients. They are taking a risk with you – as you are, with every client you take on! No wonder you find it hard to sell yourself!

Frankly, it's challenging to all but the most narcissistic individuals to engage in any kind of sales pitch for themselves and their professional skills.

THE ANSWER? LET OTHERS DO THE PRE-SELLING FOR YOU.

Here's a simple, everyday example.

You go to a conference with a featured speaker. She may be a bestselling author, but you haven't read any of her books. In fact, you have no idea why she is so highly regarded that she has been invited to this meeting and is earning big money for this appearance . . . until, that is, the master of ceremonies reads her bio and recites some of the accolades that she has received.

Another example. At a weekly Rotary luncheon with a 20-minute talk by a local businessman, the speaker's bio and credentials are delivered by the Rotary Club President or Program Director.

In both these cases, the bio materials may have been provided by the speaker, but they are delivered by someone else. The reason is more than the appearance of modesty. It's believability. Social proof.

When a speaker delivers his or her own credentials, believability goes down. When someone else does the delivering -- preferably someone known and respected -- the event starts off on a whole different foot.

This is the same reasoning behind referrals, and why they rate so high on the scale for generating leads to potential clients. You know you've hit pay dirt when the majority of referrals are second and third level . . . when the referees start with someone who doesn't necessarily know you, but has heard about you, seen you speak at a meeting or read something you've written. (Oops, there's that reference to writing and publishing again. Sounds like work. Sorry. Pretend you didn't read it here.)

HOLD THIS THOUGHT:

One of the best ways to "educate" contacts about the kind of referrals to make and what they (your contacts) can best say about your services is via a newsletter with your editorial platform. Examples of problems solved or "case histories" are golden.

2 – Aren't My Credentials and Degrees My Real Marketing?

Stop hiding behind your degrees.

"Pull" marketing vs. "Push" sales

The value of a disciplined sales process

The world has changed radically in the last thirty-five years. First it was the desktop computer. Then came the internet followed by the World Wide Web and then, increasingly, the smartphone and social media. The way people make many buying decisions has changed just as radically – but maybe not so much for professionals. There's still an eyeball to eyeball value and "chemistry," certainly at the close of the sales cycle.

UNFORTUNATELY, MOST PROFESSIONALS ARE BEHIND THE TIMES.

If your firm was around in the 1970s, you may recall that you likely had only one or two formal brochures, or maybe some reproduced white papers, perhaps pens, note pads and coffee cups with the firm's name imprinted on them. The firm's professional's credentials, degrees and awards were framed and displayed prominently on the office walls.

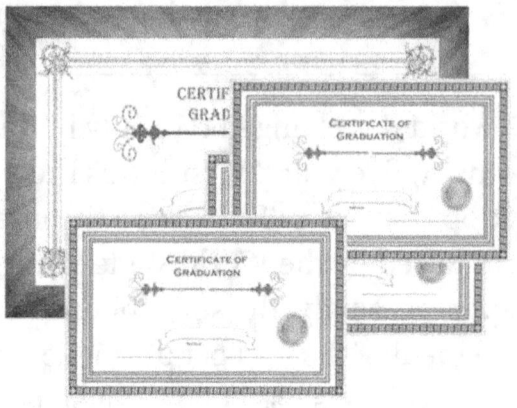

In that era, professionals could operate in an atmosphere of dignity and reserve, at least on the surface. And there was considerable reliance on credentials, diplomas, certifications and endorsements by professional associations.

Today, people who are operating according to this antiquated playbook are at a serious disadvantage.

FAST FORWARD TO TODAY'S HYPER SPEED MARKETPLACE.

By the time that you get a telephone call from a prospect, except in very rare cases, you can assume one of three things about the caller:

Caller A has checked your website and social proof (social media, professional directory or reference sites, etc.) and will likely have some specific questions about services, fees, etc. This is an example of today's "active consumer' using the tools. (That means your website and LinkedIn profile had better be top notch.) You want to take this call! Someone who does their homework and then calls you could well become a profitable, even long-term client.

Caller B is someone who has been referred by a former client, associate or someone who got your name at a cocktail party. Personal referrals are the life blood of a successful professional.

But they all are not equally valuable.

With no previous knowledge about this caller, you're starting from ground zero. They may not know your specialty, how expensive you are and for all you know they are calling to ask you to join or donate to their cause. Be sure to have your list of qualifying questions handy. You can flip a coin on this one.

Caller C is coming from the Yellow Pages. (Yes, there are still a few of them around. They are decidedly thinner!) The call from the Yellow Pages is a phone call from hell. It has always been risky for professionals to run ads in the yellow pages. Even years ago, callers responding to a yellow pages ad were likely to be in trouble and to have waited until the eleventh hour to seek help. It's probably worse today since most educated and sophisticated people use the internet and their social and professional contacts to determine who to call for help. Unless you're in the contingency fee world, this is likely to be a loser. It's a good reason to keep your competitors' phone numbers handy to pass off to this caller so you can hang up and get back to work.

These examples are admittedly over simplified. But I doubt that in any of the three examples above the prospective clients paid a lot of attention to degrees, credentials or citations from professional associations.

It's not that these testimonials to your qualifications are unimportant. Prospective clients are just focused on meeting their own important needs. They probably assume you have the credentials. They're more interested that you have the experience they need.

You should be reassured that we will be far more thorough in the next chapters. And yes, later on we'll get into some effective ways to use sheepskins and credential documents to your advantage without intimidating to prospects.

SELLING PROFESSIONAL SERVICES IS "PULLING" AS OPPOSED TO "PUSHING."

Professional sales have always incorporated a bit of mystical decision analysis. Engaging a professional nearly always gets down to developing rapport, trust and affinity between the principals. You are building a relationship, not pushing a product.

It often takes time and even a dozen or more contacts or touch points to reach conclusion or close.

In our career as direct marketing consultants we developed a disciplined sales process that covered most of what it took to draw out objections and reveal whether or not the "chemistry" of a good client relationship was present.

THE DISCIPLINED SALES PROCESS REQUIRES A NUMBER OF MARKETING TOOLS.

Here are some of the tools we have found to be helpful when conducting a successful, low-key sales dialog:

Information offerings to generate inquiries – Typically, these are variations on articles, reports, white papers, case histories or other forms of "educational" material about the services offered by the principal of the professional firm. These can take the form of downloadable or standard printed documents, booklets or even portfolios as the situation warrants. Rule of thumb: the more specific the topic, the fewer the responses . . . but the more likely the people responding will convert to clients.

Marketing-structured website – Your website is more than an "electronic brochure." It serves as a central collection point for inquiries from potential clients. It provides a structured overview of your credentials and background. It presents a clear picture of the services you provide and enough about how they are delivered so visitors to the site can determine if your services match their need/s.

The marketing toolkit can encompass some of the following as well:

An online journal – a Blog (or weblog) provides ongoing commentary on relevant single subjects so visitors to the website will be motivated to return to get your perspective.

Newsletter – This is a multi-subject document that can take several forms. Newsletters can be published weekly, bi-weekly, monthly, quarterly or simply periodically. They can be published in electronic form as "e-newsletters" and distributed through email or printed and mailed through the US Postal Service.

Membership – In some cases, a regular weekly, monthly or even a daily communication and/or training offering can be sent or published as part of a membership. The membership may be paid or unpaid.

Brochure – I list this with the caveat that in a small brochure the professional service runs the risk of downgrading (or "commoditizing") its service. More often if a printed brochure is necessary, we will recommend that services be presented in the form of inserts in a "waterfall" portfolio that can be customized to a prospect's particular needs. In some cases a large brochure in booklet form may be warranted, depending on the circumstances.

Article Reprints – News articles featuring the company or agency, white papers, citations and awards, etc. These are typically printed in black ink on white paper to "simulate" news media.

And once clients are engaged, you'll want to develop a series of customer service tools, including:

Onboarding messages – These are likely to be emails, but the official "welcome" letter may well be printed on the firm's letterhead – with a handwritten note from you -- for more impact.

Status reports and Invoices – Here's where the value of your services is subtly – perhaps not so subtly – demonstrated.

Follow-up communications – These customized messages (emails, cards, etc.) maintain the relationship with the client and continue to provide the education necessary to generate qualified referrals.

How many of these tools do you currently use? Keep the opportunities in mind as we get back to those "qualified referrals." Chapter 3 digs in more deeply.

HOLD THIS THOUGHT:

Consider this statement: "Degrees and certifications are only a foundation, a license to learn. My real education started my first years in the trenches with clients."

The first half of the statement positions credentials as matter of fact while the "in the trenches with clients" is reassuring, soft sales language.

3 - Referrals May Be The Best Source of Clients . . . But Are They Always?

Your "network" is the source of the most referrals.

The best referrals come from strangers.

Success is measured at the 2nd and 3rd levels of your network.

Most professional service firms rely heavily on word-of-mouth advertising to build and sustain their business development efforts. In doing so without a plan, these firms are delegating much of their future growth, profitability and stability to people who don't really know what kind of clients the firm needs!

Professional firms that fail to "manage" their referral process are leaving their future profits – and even the firm's viability – to chance.

Does your marketing plan have a referral and networking component?

Obviously, educating other professionals as well as clients about the firm's specialties and appropriate referrals is an important part of the firm's marketing planning.

The first step is to understand **what kinds of problems you are uniquely willing to take on and are particularly qualified to solve.** What are the firm's current strengths? What has been its history of success? What are its developing skillsets and interests?

The next step is to thoroughly understand **what kind of clients you really want**. That means analyzing the existing client base to identify the demographic and other characteristics that are most likely to represent the profile of your target market.

We'll go into this in more depth in Chapter 4. But, first let's explore the many ways referrals can be helpful to you in generating conversations with prospective clients.

A REFERRAL SYSTEM STARTS WITH YOUR NETWORK... YOUR "SPHERE OF INFLUENCE."

Are you considered an authority in your field? By whom? How many of these fans are there and where do they congregate? Do they attend meetings where your reputation might be of value to other attendees?

Do you really understand the dynamics of networking to build a referral marketing machine for your business?

Let's take a quick break here and make sure we're on the same page. When you receive a referral from a client or someone you know in the business world it's a simple relationship. We call it a "Tier One (Relationship-based) Referral. "

This is nice, but if it's the only kind of referral you receive, you're destined to fail or work yourself to death in a hand-to-mouth, mediocre business model!

PERSONAL CONTACTS ARE NOT YOUR BEST REFERRAL SOURCE OVER THE LONG HAUL.

Why? You would think these would be the most powerful referrals.

But think about some of the reasons these referrals might not be forthcoming.

If you're doing good work for a client, why would they want to refer you to a competitor? If the work you've done for them is particularly confidential, they will definitely not want to "tell the whole story."

Referrals and recommendations come with emotional strings attached and a lot depends on the relationship between the referrer and the referee (you). People might hesitate to refer you if they aren't sure you and the potential referral will "get along."

Even if you have a great relationship with clients, you may never have actually asked for referrals!

But, by far, the likely biggest impediment to gaining clients from referrals lands squarely on your marketing materials and in particular your website.

Websites are easily criticized for not clearly reflecting what you do, being too "salesy" or not being informative enough.

Experience suggests that about half of otherwise good referrals actually get "turned off" by the website!

The world has turned since the day of the Fuller Brush Man (or that pots and pans salesperson!). Sales aren't based so much on the persuasiveness of the sales representative as they are on actual knowledge about the product or service. Clients expect to be educated about products, services and business processes in order to make an informed decision.

THE BEST REFERRALS WILL START TO COME FROM PEOPLE WHO DON'T KNOW YOU.

What you really want is a continuous flow of Tier Two, Tier Three and even Tier

Four referrals. (Tier One referrals are from people you actually know. Tier Two are the people THEY know. Tier Three and Tier Four expand the circles ever more widely. It's a numbers game.)

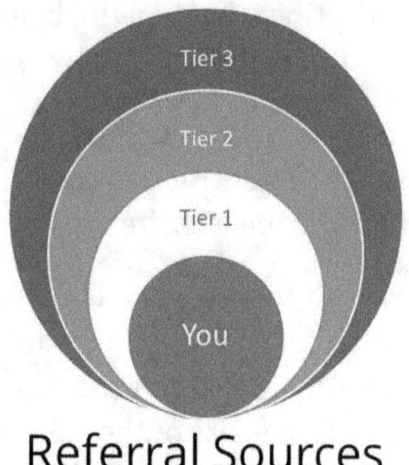

Referral Sources

Then there are the Magic Referrals that come from out of the ether . . . these are direct responses from your speaking engagements, media interviews, published articles, a published "Authority" Book, etc.

To build a real business you want to receive referrals from Tier Two and above on a continuing basis. As you circulate (networking by any other name) in your Tier One Sphere of Influence, the connections you make (i.e. **the people to whom you provide free advice and/or valuable published materials**) will carry your message into their Tier One and Tier Two networking groups. It's a whole lot easier for your Tier One people to refer an article or white paper from you than to stick their neck out and refer your services directly.

Numbers can add up fast. Let's say for the sake of illustration that your Tier One includes 200 people. And, likewise, each of these people has a Tier One of 200 people. If you manage to connect with 10% of your own group, or 20 business people . . . and each of these 20 passes your reference on to 10% of theirs, your effective Sphere of Influence now exceeds 400.

Each time you attend a meeting (with a clear plan in mind), you have the possibility of picking up another dozen or so cards and referrals. Don't just sit on those names. Send them something of value in response to what you learned at the meeting or that you know they are interested in. Make it personal!

Networking is not something you do once or twice and quit. And networking on social media, while it can be productive, is not a substitute for in-person, real time networking.

Let's look at social media more in depth.

What role does social media play in your prospecting?

The answer is, "that depends." It all depends on your target market . . . who you're selling to. Facebook is good for reaching individual consumers and even some small, local businesses. LinkedIn, however, is usually the platform of choice for professionals. Twitter and Instagram can work across a number of target audiences, consumers and businesses alike.

Your use of social media also depends on the time you have available to manage it. The more you use electronic media, the greater the time commitment just in keeping track of what was said and to whom. You quickly find yourself running additional variations on your contacts database.

Yes, there are automated tools. Hootsuite, for example, is one you've probably heard of. But all the social media management platforms require management themselves, plus a time commitment and a monthly cost.

The bottom line? Map out your referral and networking strategies carefully and integrate them deliberately into your professional marketing plan.

Chapter 6 is devoted to building that plan.

Warning. Before you jump ahead to wonder about how to keep track of all these referrals, rest assured there will be some answers coming up. Be cautious about assuming that referral management software will be useful.

Most of these programs (and there are dozens) are meant for traditional product sales teams. They often include incentives for expanding the team through affiliates or stimulating sales activity through contests and rewards. These features don't necessarily match the way you want to do business.

HOLD THIS THOUGHT:

By sharing the demographics and qualifying profile of desired clients with your existing clients and potential referral sources, you accomplish two things. You are being complimentary with them while preventing them from sending you the wrong type of referrals.

4 - How Do I Know Which Referrals Will Be Profitable?

What's the real value of a client?

Building a "best client" profile.

Building profiles for the best referral sources.

Despite your best efforts to predict which potential clients are most likely to fit the ideal profile, there are obviously things beyond your control. The only real solution is to have a process in place to spot the signs as quickly as possible.

Putting a Dollar Value on Your Average Client

A hallmark of the direct marketing world is the ability to measure response to marketing efforts, sometimes down to the penny. The most popular measure is Lifetime Customer Value (LTCV), a function of the average length of time (hopefully in terms of years) multiplied by the average annual revenue or profits from that client.

Whereas complex formulas are used to derive the LTCV for consumer products – which yield small dollar profits per sale – the LTCV of larger sales, measured in hundreds or thousands of dollars, doesn't need to be plotted down to the penny. (Rule of Thumb? A LTCV over $2,500 gives you leverage that reduces the need for a detailed LTCV analysis.)

Still, a rough understanding is useful.

Using the LTCV formula

We start with your existing client list. We'll separate it into three categories. (The first two steps will be easy.)

- Identify your long-term, **profitable** client relationships. They go into List 1.
- Put the clients that have proven to be **unprofitable** on List 3.

- Next, using your psychic powers (or "voodoo math") to extract from List 3 those clients who are close to becoming profitable and who you sincerely feel **have real potential and/or who are a proven resource for good referrals**. These clients go on List 2 . . . at least temporarily.

BUILD A "PROFILE" OF THE CLIENTS ON LIST 1.

If your clients are businesses, the demographics encompass: a. their industry (S.I.C.) category; b. geographic location (Distance you travel to work with them can be key to profitability.); c. size measured in number of employees, annual $ sales volume, etc. As part of your profile, identify the kinds of problems you solve for these companies. Don't overlook establishing what those solutions are worth to them!

If your clients are individuals – and since "companies" don't make decisions, officers (or managers) make decisions on the company's behalf — we get more detailed in the profiling process. There are five main ways to categorize people:

Demographics — What is their life situation? This includes age, sex, net worth amount of education, number of children, value of home, number of cars and type (luxury, utility, etc.) . . . all based on statistics where they live, drawn primarily from census data.

Geographics — Where are the clients located? Are they located in the U.S.? In what state or states? Are they local? If they are located some distance away, much of the sales process will likely take place over the telephone and via email. (Do you need a secure way to correspond and exchange documents with these clients?)

Technographics — How sophisticated is the prospective client in the use of electronic communications? If this seems a bit bizarre in the age of the smartphone and social media overload, rest assured that there are still millions of people (including companies and organizations) who don't use email, have trouble with social media and, surprisingly, still rely on the fax machine. If you're going to sell to these people, you will likely have to speak in their technological language.

Ergraphics (from the Greek word for "work") –These are the professional or vocational categories that includes the type of education, job title/s, industry category, trade or professional memberships, etc. that determine the need for the type of product or service you provide.

Psychographics – Unlike the life situation described by demographics, this represents the "lifestyle choices" people make, the products they purchase, the causes they support, the memberships they hold, the publications they subscribe to, etc.

As a direct marketing consultancy for over 39 years, we have designed literally hundreds of advertising and direct mail campaigns. **In every case where we used psychographics to test response, these factors proved to be 7**

to 22 times more productive as a predictor of response than other selection factors.

Here is an example of how profile testing works.

We pioneered direct bookings for a cruise ship line. Competition for passengers was stiff and getting stiffer as ship capacity increased – going from 500 to over 3,000 passengers per ship over a period of about three decades.(Today the biggest ships carry more than 6,000 passengers!) Much of this competitive war was waged on the ground in the form of direct mail. When we tested the three categories of lists we found that:

1-For compiled lists of affluent consumers (demographics), the best response was in the 1% to 2% range and average bookings were $700-$900 per person.

2-For lists of people who subscribed to publications in the travel and vacation industry (ergraphics and some assumed psychographics), response was typically *at the 1.8% to 3.2% level and the average bookings were still under $1,000.*

3-Psychographic lists (people who had inquired about or already taken a cruise) responded at the 3.7% to 6.8% level and average bookings ran between $1,100 and $1,800.

The conclusion was obvious. Despite the fact that the subscriber lists were twice as expensive as the compiled lists, the results were improved. The closer we could get to **actual interest and overt action (as opposed to theoretical and financial capability)**, the greater the response and more success we experienced in filling the staterooms.

Cost of the psychographic lists was three times that of compiled lists, but the overall mailing costs increased only incrementally. That made the increased response decidedly more profitable than either of the other two categories.

While building an accurate profile of what your ideal client looks like is a critical first step, it's only part of building your referral marketing machine.

Every bit as important as the client profiles are the profiles of the people and organizations that will send you referrals. Just as not every referral is likely to be a good prospect, not every person who refers people to you is in a position to network with the type of people you're really looking for as clients.

BUILD REFERRAL SOURCE PROFILES FOR LISTS 2 AND 3.

Finding these referral sources starts with building a profile of their characteristics.

Another more extensive example – one that surprised us!

We were consulting to a major bank based in Northern California to help them build their commercial banking centers. These centers served certain types of businesses whose annual sales typically fell between $5 million and $25 million. The owners or senior management of these businesses were frequently *skeptical of bankers and reluctant to change banks even if they weren't receiving the level of service they needed and they were receiving "better" offers from competitor banks.*

Research showed that these businesses were insecure about the workings of banks and were intimidated about entering into dialogs about their needs because of this. They also didn't think that bankers understood their business.

Our solution was to create a book about banking that avoided use of esoteric vocabulary and explained the various bank services, from accounts receivable financing to valuation of businesses, in terms that business executives could understand. We then sent a one-page direct mail letter offering the book over the signature of one of the local Calling Officers (actually financial consultants in their own right) to businesses that fit the profile of target businesses.

Response averaged between 14 and 17 percent and we mailed the non-

responders more than once over a 2 ½ year period.

But the campaign didn't stop there. (And this is the real point of the story.)

We also mailed to professional service providers who were likely to have client companies that fit our target profile. Among these were Certified Financial Advisers and CPAs.

Response from the professionals averaged over 23%!

But then came the real surprise. The bank started getting calls from officers of major corporations with annual sales of $50 million, $100 million and up. This was absolute nuts -- we hadn't even advertised to them! Businesses of this size are for all practical purposes in the banking business themselves. They use banks as servicing intermediaries. Why did they want a book aimed at less sophisticated executives?

This unanticipated (and unsolicited) response from large corporations hit almost 50%.

When we found out the reason, we re-tooled a version of the book and made a special mailing to the giant corporations and received over a 50% response. Why did they respond so strongly? ***They wanted multiple copies of the book to use in training*** *their up-and-coming managers. Who would have guessed it?*

The moral here is to be sure to turn over every corporate rock and identify every category of executive or service provider holding a position of authority or respect and who is likely to send you referrals.

This could be three people or thirty and you don't have to do it all at once. You can build these profiles as you expand your sphere of influence, allowing you to tap into their sphere of influence one, two or three steps removed. This is what makes referrals hyper-profitable.

Hold This Thought:

The first step in getting strong referrals is to know the characteristics of profitable clients. Until you analyze your client base and focus on the Tier One profitable clients, you are gambling with your practice.

5 - Selling Professional Services is a Two Phase Process

Reversing the selling role.

Authority marketing attracts qualified inquiries.

Achieving Authority status.

Earlier we covered the main psychological barriers to selling professional services. The core issue is really the stigma around "soliciting." For professionals to openly solicit client business puts them at a psychological disadvantage, painting them as needing business. It can be construed as begging.

To further illustrate my point: visualize a situation where the professional – attorney, consultant or psychologist, etc. – comes knocking on your door to inquire if you need his or her services. You would likely be hesitant to consider an engagement, even if you have a need for the services. In the back of your mind you'd be asking, "Why is she going door-to-door?"

Contrast the situation where you embark on a search for professional services, receive a recommendation or two, search some websites and decide to contact a person who seems right for your needs. The professional you've contacted maintains his or her stature while responding to your questions from a position of strength, qualifying your actual need by asking professional questions.

This start is doubly important, because beyond the initial sale, professional posture and authority will play a key role in guiding the relationship.

What does all this have to do with a two-phase Sales Process? And what is "reverse selling?"

THE SUCCESSFUL PROFESSIONAL MASTERS THE ART OF "REVERSE SELLING."

Let's start with the second point first. Reverse selling is primarily a positioning concept where you maneuver the conversation so prospects find themselves selling you on accepting them. You are "pulling" them into the sales process rather than "pushing" your services on them. ("Let me ask a couple of questions to see if the services I provide will fit your needs.")

The "two-phase" refers to making a general offer of information (white paper, report, bulletin, etc.) that is relevant to the sales topic – i.e., the problem the prospect is trying to solve. When the prospect responds by requesting the item being offered, you are entering into the second phase, the qualification phase. You are now able to step up the exchange as you respond with the item and a cover letter (or email), expanding on the topic with more detail and making a second offer.

There may be more offers and responses by mail or email before a phone conversation and subsequent face-to-face meeting is appropriate. Think of this process as a stairway starting off at the ground floor with each subsequent offer and acceptance getting you closer to the top floor, where the actual sales presentation takes place.

ANOTHER NAME FOR THIS PROCESS IS "ATTRACTION MARKETING."

This offer-response exchange, be it one step or several, is a component part of the two-phase process and is still only a part of the overall sales process.

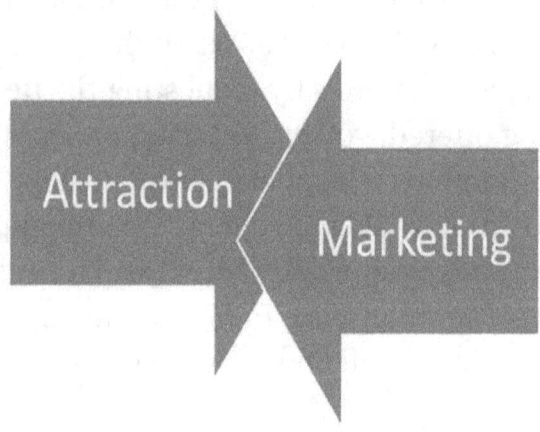

Before we leave the two-phase concept, let's drill down a little deeper into the information offers. These are also referred to as "lead magnets" because their title and substance attract people to a subject that involves (or even simply relates to) the products or services you offer. When they respond, they become a lead.

The more general or wider the topic and title, the greater the lead volume, but the "softer" and less qualified the lead will be.

(I know what you're thinking. Krueger's gone over the edge with this whole "selling isn't selling" mind game. It does seem like a lot of made-up jargon. But bear with me here. This is the real biggie!)

AUTHORITY MARKETING ATTRACTS QUALIFIED INQUIRIES.

If you become an established and recognized authority in your field, people will buy your books, read your blog posts and use your website as a research resource. They will also attend your seminars, webinars and other public appearances.

Your authority status puts you into the position to receive second and third-level referrals from these people who may never have met you face-to-face or done business with you!

How do you achieve "authority" status?

Authority status is rarely bestowed. It is earned, and usually through publishing. Consider it like producing a PhD thesis without the academic jargon designed to satisfy professors!

If you aren't a prolific writer you will have to use some of the tools and services that will compensate for your lack of skill or love of the written word. Again, if you aren't a natural born writer (some people think it's a God-given talent) it's never too late to become at least competent.

Most authorities and thought leaders are avid readers. The more you read, the better your vocabulary becomes and the easier it is to get your thoughts on paper. And technology is on your side. Software that converts the spoken word to writing is readily available.

Of course, there's no substitute for a good editor . . . who may or may not be a good proofreader. (Virginia does a lot of that editing around here!) And if English isn't your native language, you may need a translation service.

Most of your writings will take the form of articles focused on subjects associated with your profession and related markets. Having an "Authority Website" and an active blog where these articles can be published helps build credibility.

Ultimately, having your own book about the needs for (and results from) your specific services will be a major factor in your becoming a recognized authority. Of all the steps you can take, publishing your own book is probably the single most important. If you have a library of written articles and blog posts that consistently lead to coherent positions, you're already off to a good start.

We get into more detail about this in Chapter 11.

Hold This Thought:

Your first serious contact with a live prospect could be an information piece that combines your services with some key questions that evoke answers about their needs. This puts you in the position of "responding to their inquiry" as opposed to giving a sales pitch. It's a subtle difference but a strategic example of the two-phase sales process.

6- Shaping your Practice with a Good Marketing Plan

A lean and mean marketing plan.

Building a plan around your strengths.

Reaching the right audience with advertising.

"I love it when a plan comes together" is an often-repeated quote that came out of the 1980s TV show, the A Team.

It was a great line then, and it continues to work today for the well-run professional firms whose principals want to control their company's growth and profitability. There are no limits to the analogies, but our favorite is floating adrift with the currents vs. powering in the direction of profits and selected clientele. Of course, the latter requires a rudder, power source and a map.

We've already started putting that map together!

Focus on clients.

In Chapter 4 we talked about wanting clients (patients or customers, as the case may be) that would likely become repeat clients and prove to be profitable relationships. That was the lifetime value discussion. Getting through that exercise gives you a target client profile.

Focus on you.

Now let's turn around and look at you instead of the client. We need to define your (your company's) Unique Value Proposition (UVP) – how you are perceived in the marketplace. The more you understand about your UVP, the easier it will be to put together a winning marketing strategy.

The idea behind the UVP is simple. It's meant to show how you are DIFFERENT from the competition and why you are the BEST even the ONLY rational choice to solve the client's problem.

Simple as it sounds, a lot of work goes into creating a strong UVP.

Here's an example of a company name that doesn't offer any particular assistance to the prospect or project any particular brand: McKinley, a Professional Corporation.

In reading that, you have no idea of what this firm does or why it would be a better choice than the firm next door.

Consider how this might be improved by a good UVP: McKinley, Inc., Protecting Start-up Tech Companies from Intellectual Property Theft, in San Jose since 1985.

Warning: Some professional associations seek to limit the names that their members give their own firms. Check with your state's board to see the status of current restrictions or recommendations in your profession.

How to come up with the UVP?

At first, the exercise looks at what you think of yourself. After research, you may want to refine your UVP to be more reflective of marketplace realities.

Parts of the UVP exercise are situational. They take a look at facts about your competition, your resources and even local economics. (Fortunately, we have the internet and the worldwide web as a resource for conducting extensive secondary research, everything from viewing competitors' websites to analyzing the keywords that people use when searching for information that relates to your specific products or services.)

Parts of the exercise are more subjective. A SWOT analysis, for example, estimates your firm's Strengths, Weaknesses, Opportunities and Threats -- from an internal as well an external perspective.

(We are big believers in SWOT analyses. If you haven't done one lately, let us know you'd like our free SWOT report. We have more than one version, depending on the business you are in.)

When the research is done, the resulting UVP is typically a sentence or maybe just a phrase. But it's not just words. Your UVP works very hard to **identify a need** that exists in your target marketplace, is **easy to remember**, and **strikes an emotional chord**. You will be using your UVP in all of your marketing materials!

Your plan matches client needs with your firm's strengths.

A Cautionary Note: The best plans get changed in order to adapt to changing realities of the marketplace.

"No plan survives contact with the enemy."

Most of us are familiar with that famous quote. (It has been attributed to Colin Powell, Dwight Eisenhower, Sun Tzu and even Napoleon Bonaparte, but it likely originated in the 1800s with Field Marshal Helmuth Karl Bernhard Graf von Moltke. The original German text was considerably longer, as you might expect.) No matter which version of this proclamation you choose to accept, the message is clear.

No plan is perfect and planning is an ongoing exercise.

Unlike a Business Plan, which tends to be more enduring and focused on longer-term activities, the Marketing Plan is dynamic. It is comparable to a battle plan. It is the day-to-day guide to how you will spend your resources – time, money and creative energies. In the direct marketing context you have the opportunity to test tactics and, in some cases, strategies.

THE PLAN'S FLAWS WILL BE REVEALED EARLY ON.

We want to build options and feedback mechanisms into the plan. These can guide us in making adjustments and changes that jettison underperforming assets and redirect resources in more productive ways.

Your marketing plan is the central point of coordination among the various media promotions and the messages these promotions are designed to carry.

WHAT STRATEGIES WILL YOU BE TESTING?

Strategies are the "high-level" long-term concepts or goals that you will use to improve the flow and income potential of your clients. Since this book is focused on referrals, some marketing strategies for referrals might be:

- **Strategy**: Generate more referrals in your local marketplace from current clients. (*penetration*)
- **Strategy**: Emphasize one outstanding skillset or characteristic of your practice not shared by any of your competitors. (*differentiation*)
- **Strategy**: Introduce new technology that will allow you to lower prices or speed up results and thus be more competitive. (*innovation*)

The SWOT analysis will give you some good ideas about strategies to consider. Once you decide on a strategy, or perhaps two, you'll begin to examine the best way or ways to reach that goal. Here's where various promotional tactics come into play.

Every marketing initiative will be different, but will likely use a combination of the same tools or tactics. Which should you be considering for your referral plan?

DON'T OVERLOOK CLASSIC MARKETING TOOLS AND TACTICS.

Traditional marketing methods are still as important as ever. Before you include a single one as part of your marketing plan, though, you'll want to examine it closely to uncover how it might fit with your target market, your market's unique concerns, and your firm's ability to provide the appropriate, personalized solution.

- Advertising – Print (Magazines, Newspapers, etc.), electronic (Radio, Television), digital
- Collateral – Printed brochures, flyers, business cards

- Direct Mail – to businesses, consumers, organizations, etc.
- Newsletters, e-newsletters, podcasts
- Networking – Meetings, seminars, events, etc.
- Joint Ventures & Partnerships – Teaming up with others serving the same markets
- Publishing – Articles, books, columns and white papers, etc.
- Public Relations – News releases, feature stories, public speaking, interviews, etc.
- Professional Association leadership
- Pro bono work
- Sponsorships – Arts, sports activities, etc.

In the last decade some (not all) of the classic methods have lost place to the internet and the associated digital media as advertising and content delivery methods of choice.

DEFINITELY INCORPORATE ELECTRONIC OR ONLINE MEDIA.

The website is at the hub of this activity. More than just an electronic brochure, your website is both a distribution system for marketing messages and your central collection point and filter (or "lead funnel") for the resulting inquiries and responses.

Your website is one marketing option that you can't skip! We will feature it in more depth in Chapter 11.

As already mentioned, in its early years the internet promised a way for the small business community to level the marketing playing field. In the ensuing years, however, we have seen corporate advertising strategies and big budgets shift from the typical offline media to electronic platforms. The bar has been raised on free and inexpensive online media, but there are still opportunities.

Many options are available for you to consider and combine. I expect this (potentially incomplete) list of digital marketing methods is familiar to you:

- eMail – Directed to clients, prospective clients and other target markets (e.g., referral sources)
- Social Media – Active presence on LinkedIn, Twitter, Facebook, Instagram, YouTube, etc.
- Blogging – Proprietary blog posts, guest blog posts, etc.
- Webinars – Educational or promotional, often with partners
- Podcasting – Pre-recorded talks and interviews usually available by subscription
- Content Marketing – Educational and instructional material, both public and private
- Article marketing – Professional topics, White papers
- Website/s – Focal Points for target markets, inquiries & leads harvesting
- Search Engine Optimization – SEO applied to all online contributions

NO MATTER THE MEDIUM, PROFESSIONAL SERVICES MARKETING REQUIRES DISCIPLINE.

You may understand the needs and motivations of prospective clients or referral sources. But your messages reaching out to them require editorial judgement!

We've said it before, but it bears repeating: marketing professional services is not the same as "hawking a consumable" in broad media ads!

Just like financial advertising, which is actually regulated by the SEC to cull out deceptive language, when it comes to professional services marketing your clients will expect restraint and low-key terminology. Using a lot of superlatives or hyperbole, and making any sort of promise of results, are not advised and may draw unwelcome attention from the FTC.

Keep your eye on the basics.

Everything you do in planning your marketing must be focused on the profile of your market and be based on your Unique Value Proposition (UVP), the foundation of your brand.

(Actually, you may remember back to the days when the UVP was the USP, or "Unique Sales Proposition." This reflected the earlier emphasis on life in the trenches where making the sale was the objective. These days we talk about providing value to the customer. The ultimate goal of generating revenue hasn't changed, though!)

After over fifty years of direct marketing history, **three factors** continue to have the biggest impact on response to your marketing message.

1. The Target Market – List, Readers, Listeners, Audience, etc. **At least 50% of the success** of a campaign is controlled by your ability to reach the right people who are most likely to be interested in your message.

2. Your Offer – What are you offering and how you are suggesting they buy (one-time purchase, retainer, etc.) accounts for **25-40%** of your success. In the professional setting

the offer might be the purchase or gift of a book, a complimentary consultation, even a free dinner along with an educational seminar. The actual contract could include payment up front, a down payment followed by regular progress payments, or a retainer. These features are all part of the offer.

3. <u>The Creative Execution</u> – Another **10%-15%** depends on how creatively you've crafted the message, the copy and artwork, etc. (I know this is disappointing to many, especially people who value creativity, but these results have been proven over and over again in many thousands of tests.)

Think of it this way. You can send a cleverly-crafted message, enhanced by beautiful artwork, to a list of people who have no need of (or even interest in) your services, and get approximately zero response.

Contrast that with a modest message, executed with little or no artwork, but sent to an audience that has proven need for the service. You will get response!

If you have a winning offer but feel there is evidence that response can be improved, that's when you fine tune the list and test variations on the offer for some incremental improvement. In other words, creativity in execution won't save a losing product or service (only the list can do that), but it can accelerate response to a proven winning approach.

Your Marketing Plan encompasses all of this . . . what you do, whom you do it to (and with) and when and how you do it. All of these factors will impact your success or lack of it. And all of it is changeable and incrementally testable, assuming your resources (think money, enthusiasm, etc.) hold out. So, while you want to build flexibility into your market planning, it behooves you to get it right the first time . . . or as close to being right as you can.

Hold This Thought:

If you don't have a real Marketing Plan for your business, it's time to start building one. If you are a small firm or a solo practitioner, keep it simple . . . at least to begin with. If you already have a plan, now is the time to review it and eliminate (or move to lower priority) any activities that won't produce qualified referrals.

(Hint: Your collateral materials, white papers, article reprints, client questionnaires and transcripts of talks, etc., all have "staying power" with clients and prospects at a controllable cost that advertising simply can't match.)

7 - The Professional's Sales Process and The Role of Each Stage

Step by step to closing the sale.

Sales funnel or sales process?

Matching media to your sales process.

HOLD YOUR FIRE UNTIL YOU SEE THE WHITES OF THEIR EYES.

Closing sales is more of a risky business today than it was twenty or thirty years ago. If you believe that the internet has given you some new and inexpensive sales tools you would be correct. But the internet is a double-edged sword. It provides the buyer – your customer – with a huge selection of tools for evaluating your products and services and comparing them to your competition.

You need a process that will keep the prospect engaged with you long enough to make a good decision.

This chapter is about the professional sales process or, as it's sometimes called, the sales sequence or the sales funnel. In business there is a definite order to the selling process and its corollary, the buying process.

<u>Fact</u>: Sales are the real "bottom line" of a business.

(Heard that before?)

Selling can be straightforward and uncomplicated. But, particularly in a professional setting, it often is complex and time consuming. For example, a consultant seeking an assignment may find a number of "corporate teams" – each representing a different department in the prospect company – being involved in the decision. This may require the consulting firm to field its own team of people with appropriate expertise to go head-to-head with the buyers' teams.

Even in simpler circumstances, it takes several contacts (or "touchpoints") with a prospective customer (client or patient) before the actual sale is completed.

- Some of these factors you can control.
- Some of them you can anticipate and affect.
- Some you can only react to when they occur.

And the longer your sales cycle, the more complex and challenging your sales process is likely to be.

In every case, however, you can improve the odds for a favorable outcome by carefully analyzing and structuring your sales process **to meet the expectations of the buyer**.

That is, by identifying each contact and event leading to the sale, and examining the factors affecting it, you can select the right media then create the appropriate communications to guide the prospect through each step in the sequence. Each touchpoint or contact where questions arise and, in response, answers are provided, represents a step in the process.

<u>Fact</u>: The only real objective of each step in the sales process is to reach agreement to proceed to the next step in the sequence.

Each step focusses on answering a question, satisfying a need or dealing with a particular objection, taking you one step closer to the ultimate decision.

Before we get into the mechanics of the sales process there are two other terms that describe the progression through different lenses.

First, here is how a field sales office or a sales representative might view it.

Sales Process = Sales Funnel

The concept here is that prospects requesting information or showing interest in other ways actually enter a "funnel process" where curiosity seekers are weeded out while real prospects are presented with a series of messages and offers and drawn toward a consummated sale.

Funnel Selling

This viewpoint is almost universally shared by people in the Internet Marketing community, the modern-day mail order industry. Our problem with this is that, like the apple falling from Newton's tree, it implies a certain amount of (gravity induced?) inevitability.

When looked at through a different lens,

Sales Process = Sales Pyramid

Some see at it as more like a pyramid where the path to sales is compared to building blocks, overcoming objections (toward a pinnacle, working against gravity?) to a successful conclusion. This is not a popular comparison, probably because it implies heavy lifting . . . not the sort of thing that appeals to most sales professionals.

Pyramid Selling

Regardless of which analogy you use, the sales process includes all the steps that lead to the sale. Examine each step in the process and decide the best way to accomplish the objective of that step.

Sales Process = Sales Sequence

A marketing communications strategist looks at the process as a sequence of communications!

- What kind of questions will need to be resolved before a decision can be reached?
- Who are the participants in the decision making, including influencers?

- What "language" do the participants speak? Operational, financial, customer experience, etc.?
- What medium best advances the sale at each step?
- What protocols are in place at the prospective client company that dictate or restrict any particular medium? (For example, email attachments may not be deliverable.)

The communications (again, sales touchpoints) can include phone calls, mailings, white papers, webinars, emails, in-person meetings, etc.

You've surely heard the "rule" that it takes 7 contacts for a sale to take place. In fact, the number for a big-ticket professional sale may be greater! Your job as rainmaker for your firm is to help figure out **the optimum order and medium for each touch point**.

Here is an example of a traditional, though overly simplified, sales sequence.

Sales Sequence

1. Print Ad

The ad is designed to generate inquiries for a new service via a specific type of response. An offer of a booklet or white paper is included in the ad. Responders will be self-selecting.

2. Inbound Phone Call

The prospect responds by phone. The call is taken by a customer service representative (In a small firm this is likely to be your office manager.) who collects name, title and company and has the chance to ask one or two initial qualifying questions to determine level and nature of interest.

3. eMail

The next logical touchpoint is an email sent by the professional office to acknowledge the contact, confirm contact info, and set up the next step. The acknowledgment email will list the information needed to make that next contact most productive.

4. Fulfillment Package

If the initial ad offered printed information, the fulfillment package is personalized as much as possible, and delivered at this point. The package provides important background for the next contact.

5. Outbound Phone Call

This call is designed to further qualify the prospect and set or confirm an appointment.

6. Initial In-person Contact

Meeting the prospect face-to-face for the first time gives you the opportunity to meet and establish rapport with both the principal buyer and any others who will influence the sale. If that meeting takes place at the prospect company, it gives you the chance to see firsthand their working environment and tasks as they relate to your services. You need to get agreement on the next step.

7. Follow-up emails

Every step requires a follow-up that summarizes progress, poses questions that help move the conversation further, and confirms the next step.

8-12, etc. - Subsequent In-person Sales Visits (where possible and appropriate)

It is possible to come to an agreement at the initial meeting, but often the professional sale will require more than one visit. The goal of each subsequent visit is to review the prospect's needs (and level of urgency), make any required demonstrations, and ultimately obtain a signed commitment.

In reality, these eight steps are only about half or even a third of the touchpoints required in the normal complex business-to-business sale. In particular there are likely to be many more email and telephone contacts along the way, each of which will have a particular objective in the process. All should be treated as serious and strategic steps toward the overall goal of meeting the prospect's needs and expectations.

Right about now you may find yourself asking, "Can any of this be automated?"

The answer is, "Yes, but very carefully."

Professionally drafted "core" messages – that include client profile language and firm UVP -- can easily be customized and sent out at the appropriate point in the sequence. The key words here are "professionally drafted." Not everyone is a good marketing copywriter.

EACH STEP IN THE SALES SEQUENCE "SELLS" ONLY THE NEXT STEP.

Keep in mind that each step in this (overly simplified) example of a sequence is focused on selling only the next step in the process. An attempt to skip a step or use a medium that can't accomplish the objective will lengthen the sales cycle and may even lose the sale.

A properly-designed sales sequence is flexible and can be modified to mirror the prospect's "Buying Sequence."

In a consumer sale, even an elaborate one like a home or investment, there are likely to be fewer steps than in a large business environment, simply because there are fewer people involved. In most cases, even though several contacts may be necessary to close the sale, they will all be with the decision maker(s) and will progress in an orderly fashion from introductory conversation through to closure.

In a consumer sales situation, the influencer can be a spouse, parent or even a child. And for these prospects, "social proof" like online testimonials or recommendations of authority can play an important part in their decision to buy.

In large business settings, we often spend more time "selling" to people who aren't directly involved with our service than we do with actual users. Each "influencer" or "approver" may have a specific job function and/or a personal agenda. By "approving" the product or service as a logical solution to the company's need, they are lending their credibility to your recommendations. For these approvers, in particular, we need to be clear as to the value our services deliver, not so much how we deliver it.

Sales opportunities in a large company may result from an internal referral, possibly from someone in another department. That person may or may not wind up on the buying team. Keep track of those referrals!

Danger: The sales sequence is subject to unanticipated events, changes in priorities, etc.

It's one thing to have an elegant and synchronous sales process on paper, but day-to-day practice may be different!

Your written process is really an outline. The actual process is likely to be disrupted by a prospective client's "Buying

Process" as well as their staffing structure, personalities and need for your service. These days it's common for every industry to experience sudden changes in legal requirements, staff make-up, competition, or technology.

Hold This Thought:

The Professional Sales Process is more than simple conversations about sales and objections. While the objective for each step is to get agreement to proceed to the next step, the role of collateral material is crucial in moving the process along. The time to design or modify your Sales Process and typical variations in the sequence is now, before your next appointment.

8 -- Building Your Brand and Selling into "The Long Game"

Your brand vs. a logo.

Who builds your brand?

Building on your Unique Value Proposition.

What is this "brand" thing all about? We're not Coca Cola or Pricewaterhouse-Coopers. Just how important is it for a professional services firm to have a brand anyway?

These questions – and the skepticism they convey – are not untypical of many professionals, especially smaller firms and solo operators.

Most newcomers to the concept of building a brand put the cart before the horse and adopt a subjectively designed logo in the mistaken belief that the design becomes their brand.

Wrong, wrong, wrong!

It may be a clever design but it isn't your brand. It's just a clever design that may actually detract from your real brand . . . whatever that actually turns out to be.

Here's a quick test. If a client or business associate asks you to describe your logo, do you have a good explanation? If not, you are positioning yourself as an amateur thinker in the business context.

A PURPOSEFULLY DESIGNED LOGO CAN BECOME A POWERFUL ASSET.

Once you know your position in the marketplace, what you stand for and what you want your brand to be -- once you've done the research, the analysis and made some important decisions about the direction you are heading – once you (and your designer) know what brand the logo is meant to represent -- THEN you will be better able to come up with a strong, productive design.

Warning: The logo should come last in the process.

No matter who you are, a large, medium or small firm, if you are at all active in the marketplace, you already have a brand. It may be blurred or largely unrecognizable. And, having no brand is the biggest brand of all, shared by thousands of other invisible firms.

Brand is really all about "positioning" yourself in the marketplace, differentiating your services from the competition.

The word goes back to the era of the branding iron which was used to burn a rancher's "brand" into the flesh of cattle or other livestock. The purpose for ranchers and herders was to denote ownership or to restrict movement of designated livestock.

Today, a brand is really just a combination of reputation of a person, company or product and what the customer or consumer in your market thinks it is. You might want to ponder that last sentence . . .

"Your brand is whatever the consumer thinks it is!"

With the growth of commerce and codification of products with "brand names," the meaning of "brand" has morphed into an intangible concept. David Ogilvy defined it as "the intangible sum of a product's attributes."

This creates a challenge. Not only do you need to conceptualize and claim your brand, you must continually perform and project it. A well-crafted brand is with you wherever you go and, in your absence, it represents you for better or worse.

(Keep that in mind as you grapple with coming up with a logo design. If that logo doesn't engender **a natural association** with your brand, you will have to work hard -- and spend precious resources -- to establish the connection.)

BACK TO THE DRAWING BOARD FOR THE UNIQUE VALUE PROPOSITION

If your brand is to be unique, who you are as a personality, the way you deliver your services as well as for whom you provide them must be cohesive and maintained consistently.

In many respects it is more important for you as a professional to have a memorable brand than if you were a line of cosmetics or a box of cereal. That's because you depend on referrals – often from people you've never met – and it's critical that you get referrals that are a fit.

Your brand is pivotal in helping people think of you when presented with referral situations that suit your objectives and capabilities.

Your brand precedes you and represents you even when you can't be present. It's more than just a string of words or a clever, exotic design. Think of it as a 3D hologram, a mental picture someone has of you and your firm.

Here are some ways of differentiating your firm to build your brand.

- Focus on a specialized (rare?) service.
- Define the industry or situation where this service is critical.
- Clarify the size of organizations you specialize in.
- Become known for consistently unique results.

  Our firm, for example, is known for high performance direct mail lead-generation. We consistently achieve dramatic results (typical response rates of 20% to 60% and even 90%). We achieve these results because we immerse our design team in the workings of the target markets and the skillset of our clients' professional sales teams. One of the reasons we can achieve these results across a wide swath of businesses is our unique engineering heritage and long history of working in an unusually large number of industries.
- Can the level of expertise of your staff be a differentiating factor?

- The overall size of your firm, including branch office locations, can be a unique point of appeal.
- Capitalize on the specialized reputations of a group of clients as a differentiating factor.
- Use a unique service idea as a differentiator. ("Results within 24 hours.")
- Along the same lines, use a guarantee of results, maybe even a money back guarantee.
- Use a unique, highly visible success story as noteworthy or even famous signature accomplishment.

There are at least a dozen more ways a professional firm can differentiate itself. Some may be subtle variations on one of these ten examples or actually be new ideas altogether.

This all reminds me of a story to illustrate this point about differentiation.

Years ago we were called in to collaborate on a client project that sold high-tech measurement instruments. In this case the product was an electronic device that measured the vibrations of cable (wire rope) connections. It was a radio-like receiver connected by electronic cable to a hand-held wand.

Prior to introduction of this device, when cables like those holding up the spans of a bridge needed to be tested, they had to be disconnected one at a time. A spring-like device was attached in the gap, and the stress was measured by a spring-driven dial.

This was a long, tedious and imperfect method of measuring important construction assemblies.

The client had substituted a simpler method. Tapping the connected cable with a small hammer generated a vibration frequency that was recorded by the hand-held wand. The frequency indicated the load. This job could be done in minutes, dramatically cutting costs.

The public relations agency had come up with a scenario that featured a bikini-clad woman atop one of the Golden Gate

Bridge Towers holding the wand against the safety cable. What struck us was the seriousness with which everyone -- except one member of the client's team -- was taking this outrageous, nonsensical, even desperate attempt at branding. Our challenge was finding a gracious way to exit the project.

The point of this story is that a lot of goofy stuff goes on in the advertising/P.R. world that passes for creativity in search of memorability!

Lending our expertise to promoting this excellent product with a foolish theme would have damaged the credibility of the client and sullied our reputation as well. Fortunately, the client saw this in time. (The PR guy went on to even bigger things!)

To be real, a brand must be both true and believable lest it backfire or just fizzle out.

Branding to represent your position in the marketplace is a serious subject that warrants research as well as careful consideration. Frivolous attempts at branding may result in temporary publicity or notoriety, but the result can be a negative reputation that is a brand you don't want attached to your firm or your client.

HOLD THIS THOUGHT:

Your brand is not your logo! Your logo is simply a visual device that triggers a recollection (recognition) of your brand. Your brand is your clients' and your prospects' opinion of your company – whatever that is. The first step toward building your brand is analyzing your UVP. Your UVP is a critical factor in determining who will refer clients to you and what they will say about you.

9 - Using Direct Mail to Generate Leads and Stimulate Referrals

Understanding this powerful medium.

A campaign starts with the calculator.

The cost per unit of mail vs. value of responses.

If you've gotten this far, you probably have the courage to keep reading through to the end. These last three chapters are as challenging as they are important!

We're starting with direct mail marketing. You will have recognized by now that it is our favorite medium.

And perhaps this prompts a question:

"Why in the world would anyone want to use 'snail mail' to promote their services or products when everyone knows that email is faster and cheaper?"

The answer is one word: "Response!"

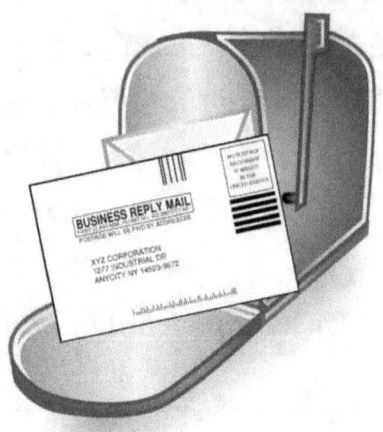

When used strategically and correctly, direct mail is one of the most powerful communications tools available to you.

The following statistics for 2018 were reported by the Direct Marketing Association (DMA) *Response Rate Report 2018*:

- Direct mail response rates were 4.9% for **prospect lists** in 2018. This is significantly higher than in

2017 and the highest since the report started in 2003.
- The response rate for **house lists** in 2018 was 9%, nearly double from the previous year!
- Direct mail pulls a higher response rate than any digital direct marketing medium, ranging from about five to nine times greater than that of email, paid search, or social media.

And a couple more statistics that are helpful in explaining our confidence in direct mail:

- While overall direct mail volume continues to decline, this means less competition in the mailbox. People notice their mail messages and recognize them when they see them later in different formats.
- The average person is getting well over 100 emails a day, and spends less than 2 minutes on each one. A direct mail piece keeps the recipi-

ent engaged longer and provides something to refer to later.
- After receiving a professional firm's marketing message, the first step for around 80% of people will be to visit the firm's website.

Let's use these statistics as a starting point for exploring the use of direct mail by professionals to promote their products and/or their services.

Before we get too deep into the subject, though, let's clarify what is meant by "direct mail."

Direct Mail vs. Mail Order

Mail Order is a method of distribution that may or may not include using "Direct Mail" as an advertising medium. As an example, you can order a product by responding to a phone call or online by clicking on a link on your computer or your smartphone. Your product is delivered electronically (digital products) or by FedEx or UPS or the US Postal Service (USPS).

Mail Order is a process for making a purchase and has become a generic term for this means of purchasing goods or services regardless of which media are used and whether or not the mail is involved in either the ordering or fulfillment.

Direct Mail Advertising is most used by industry as a two-stage, lead-generating medium that makes an offer and provides a choice of ways to respond, by mail, email or telephone (inbound telemarketing). It is also a mainstay of non-profit groups asking for support in the form of donations or specific actions.

Direct mail, texting, email and recorded phone messages are all in the same category as smoke signals or Tweets -- that is, they are communications media.

One of the main advantages of using direct mail as a communications medium is that you are designing the medium and not being confined to some number of characters or electronic blips on a digital screen. Not to be overlooked is the fact that direct mail is a physical and visual medium as well as an intellectual one.

And the results you can achieve using direct mail are significant. Some campaigns we have launched have received 30%, 40%, even 60% response. A couple even reached 90%!

Direct Mail format categories

Direct mail isn't just letters. Here are some of the main format categories of direct mail:

- Statement Stuffers – Miniature flyers or brochures that accompany a receipt or statement, and that contain a mail order ordering coupon or toll-free phone offer.
- Self-Mailer Brochures – From postcards to folded broadsides and catalogs, these typically arrive in your mailbox without envelopes.
- Letter Ensembles – The classic direct mail "package" includes an envelope, cover letter, brochure

(printed informational piece) and response card or envelope.
- Dimensional Mailings – These are "premium "packages that include objects of value and are often shipped by UPS.
- Special Containers -- A variety of existing containers for special contents with established carriers of important messages, from telegrams and mailing tubes to Priority Mail and FedEx envelopes

One of our most successful dimensional mailings, for example, cost $23 for each package mailed out!

Whoa!

(Surely that's your reaction, just like everybody else's!)

Hang on . . . we only needed 10% response to be profitable! That's because the average responding company purchased over $280,000 as a result!

THE BOTTOM LINE: YOU DON'T CARE ABOUT THE COST OF THE MAILING.

Speed readers wait . . . This is too important. Read it and burn it into your creative brain:

You. Don't. Care. About. The. Cost. Of. The. Mailing!

The real way to evaluate the effectiveness of a mailing is the level of response and the profitability that results. (Back to Chapter 4 and the LTCV.)

A simple example (for illustration purposes only):

- A mailing is estimated to cost $15,000. That seems like a lot to you.
- Response to this same mailing brings in over $500,000 of new business at 20% net profit.
- Would this make sense to consider as a marketing investment? Absolutely! (Many sophisticated mail order giants will actually lose money on their first response of 1-2%. But they more than make it up in bounce-back mailing to those who

do respond because the reorder rate is over 25% and the average order might be 3 or 4 times the initial one.)

When promoting high-end products or services (like those of professionals), the greater average revenue per typical sale justifies the more expensive unit of mail.

A lot of executives have been brainwashed by the 2% myth. They just can't bring themselves to see a higher response rate. If you've heard this myth, now's the time to get past it!

The DMA statistics listed earlier show the average consumer response is now over 5%. And our results over decades have been consistently higher.

Admittedly there is a lot more to calculating profitability. The place we usually start is with the cost of the service, the Lifetime Value of a Client (LTCV)* and the average sale. Add to this the structure of the sales process and the length of the average sales cycle.

What you're looking for is a way that a mailing campaign can alter the playing field and increase both the volume of sales and accelerate bookings to increase penetration into the most lucrative parts of your market.

Here is where we operate differently from most agencies and direct mail shops.

Once again, we take a strategic view. We don't stop at mail response, leads. We're concerned with conversion to sales. That means conducting a thorough needs assessment and sales process analysis, which includes working directly with the sales team. (That could just be you!)

We even make sales calls with members of the client's sales team where it is appropriate. We analyze the structure of the client's sales process and the internal environment of the client's target companies. We attempt to identify cultural pressures and personal motivations of the clients so we can craft an offer that will induce them to respond and ultimately convert to buyers.

Important point: If the answers and the numbers don't add up, we decline the assignment which is why we don't do proposals. We take a three-phase approach that starts by funding our needs analysis. You, as a professional consultant might want to take a look at this concept. We've covered it at both <u>ConsultantsMarketingMachine.com</u> and <u>www.JosephKrueger.com</u>.

This is more in-depth research than most agencies will undertake. It's also a greater upfront investment than companies are accustomed to making. Moreover, most of the advertising agency creative teams have little if any real outside sales experience.

However, the results we consistently achieve more than justify the process with a greater R.O.I. While a great many of our dimensional mailing campaigns have won most of the major industry awards for creativity as well as results, our creative planning starts with a strategy that wherever possible is designed to "alter the playing field."

(Remember that $23 package mentioned above? It started out at 40% response and ultimately reached over 80%. The companies that responded bought an average of $625,000 worth of our client's products and services – 3 times more than we had planned for.)

"WELL, LET'S TRY SOME DIRECT MAIL TO SEE IF IT WORKS."

Oops, that doesn't sound like we're off to the right start!

If you catch yourself approaching direct mail this way, keep these three things in mind:

1. Direct mail is among the most expensive per unit cost of most forms of advertising.
2. The ability of direct mail to garner an emotional (as well as an intel-

lectual) response can have a major backlash.

3. The direct response capability means you have the ability to test your brainstorms on a small scale before taking a big leap.

All too often this approach consists of a "creative idea" converted into a mailing that produces unsurprisingly dismal results.

Direct mail has the mistaken reputation of being an inexpensive advertising workhorse. A do-it-yourself advertising game. But the medium's true value emerges only when it can be managed to become **a predictable activity that generates customers at a price you can afford.** And often, it is a brilliant way to increase penetration and position competition.

So whether you're thinking in terms of "a few thousand dollars," or even "a few hundred thousand dollars," just take a step back. Direct mail is a lot more complex than it appears. And the artwork, the creative design, is the LAST thing you do!

Direct mail isn't a medium for amateurs to experiment with. The good news is there is a large body of knowledge and proven rules to guide us, based on the billions of dollars that millions of companies have spent over many decades. Before you break any of these historic rules, be sure you know the rule you're breaking and have a darn good reason for doing so.

Sound planning for direct mail doesn't start with a given budget. It certainly doesn't start with the cost of the direct mail piece. It actually starts with a look at the endgame: the bottom line of profits and the customer.

So it's back to the marketing drawing board . . . and the calculator.

- Which clients are really profitable, or could be profitable? (That was your List 1 from Chapter 4.)

- How much is a good client worth over the long term (Lifetime Customer Value - LTCV)?
- How much of that value are you willing to spend to get and keep a new client?

How many potentially profitable clients reside within your service area?

- What is the geographical reach for your service?
- How densely populated is the target area?
- Is your list "universe" large enough to justify a series of mail tests?
- What external factors could impact the growth potential of your likely audiences?

Have you already developed a defined sales process for acquiring and retaining new clients? How will this mailing work as part of this sales process? (See reference to sales process in Chapter 7.)

- Can you track and measure leads, lead conversion rates, subsequent cross-sell and upsell results for your various target audiences?
- Do you have previous documented experience (statistics) with direct mail?
- How do your previous direct mail results compare with those from other firms?
- Do you know what is working for your competitors . . . and how well?

How many new clients can you handle? How many do you want to book over the next year?

- What is your historical conversion rate from inquiry to prospect to client?
- What kind of response do you need to meet your sales goals? What percentage of response can you realistically expect from this campaign?
- Since the mailing list is the single most important factor in the suc-

cess of a mailing, do you plan to test different lists in each mailing?
- With the offer being the second most important factor, can you test different offers as well?
- What size test cells will return a statistically reliable result that you can use to project future results?

Armed with answers to these questions, you can begin to put together your direct mail plan, mail quantities, budget, timetable and your project management timeline of tasks. (Check out the diagram in the Appendix for more detail.)

Once you know who you are mailing to (lists) and what kind of proposition you will be making (your offer), it's time to start your creative. If you've already begun, before knowing these things, you could be hurting your potential response. Maybe it would be a good idea to go back and take a new look to make sure you're appealing in the right way to the right audience.

As for the creative tasks, there are just too many variables to cover all the possibilities in this small book. We are considering a book devoted to the creative process. In the interim we will be **building selected materials and components of the creative process** and making them available to our website readers. Get on one of our lists to be the first to get announcements of these bonus materials.

By the way, the list of questions above is meant to help guide the development of a direct mail marketing campaign. The questions could just as well be used to develop nearly ANY marketing effort. Keep them in mind!

P.S. Sorry if this comes across as complex. Direct mail done right can be a very predictable and productive adventure. But it's anything but simple!

HOLD THIS THOUGHT:

The Direct Mail medium is the most powerful tool that is fully under your control. Unfortunately, most people do not understand how it really works and they misuse it.

In our experience, something like 80-85% of direct mail efforts either fail or fail to perform profitably . . . mostly because they are created by amateurs or seen as "throwaways" from the outset.

Contrast this with the fact that professionally produced and executed mail becomes a predictable source of response with a predictable return on investment.

Used correctly, direct mail can drive referrals to your business and open doors to organizations and effect introductions to key people. You control the message, the timing, the format, everything. You will be judged on all of the elements.

Want more on direct mail? Head to Joe's website and download your full-color **bonus infographic**.

Direct Mail Checklist for B2B Marketers

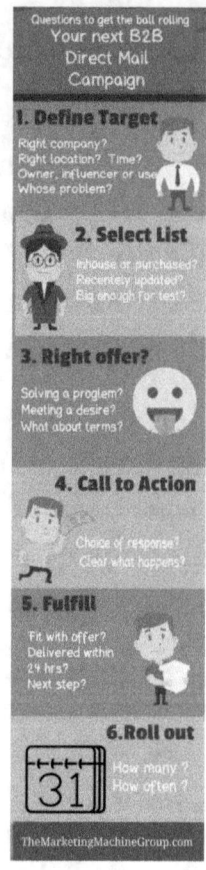

!

10 - Feeding Your Referral Engine

Putting it in writing.

Reaching multiple audiences.

Setting priorities for your time.

In order for people to refer you, they need to KNOW you . . . or, maybe even better, TO HAVE HEARD ABOUT YOU from someone they respect. Here are three ways for you to break through the anonymity of the marketplace and get your name (your brand) out there. At the same time, remember your goal is not just to be known, but also to generate lists of prospects and referral sources.

Let's start with one of our favorites.

Writing

Yep, we're back to the written word. Like it or not your professional reputation rests on the quantity and quality of your ideas. While the sound of your voice can fade into obscurity within 72 hours, your written words (or recorded words!) can live on and fuel referrals for months and years to come.

Ignore this opportunity at your peril.

Here are some ways to boost your career through writing:

- Publish expert content on your website. See Chapter 11.
- Offer original content as a guest blogger on sites that reach your target market.
- Write a column for local newspaper or select industry magazine/s.
- Polish your LinkedIn profile and participate in appropriate LinkedIn groups.
- Publish your book (and give it away). Yes, your book, see Chapter 12.
- Host a LinkedIn Group.
- Interview other experts; write it up as an article or another book.

- Write articles for article directories, trade publications, local newsletters, etc.
- Publish press releases (about the firm, about your book, about your article, your podcast, etc.)
- Publish your own newsletter targeted to your prospective clients.
- Provide customized articles as gifts for subscribers of newsletters, etc.
- Draft a cover memo and deliver any of the above to your current client referral sources.

And more ways to become known and referable . . .

Giving Informal Talks, Conducting Interviews and Serving on Panels

- Be a webinar participant.
- Give a radio interview as an expert.
- Narrate a SlideShare presentation.
- Host a podcast.
- Be a resource for reporters (HARO.com – Help a Reporter Out).

- Be a guest on a podcast.
- Give talks to local college classes.

Delivering Major Presentations

- Host a live webinar or online workshop.
- Jointly host a webinar.
- Promote yourself as a guest speaker.
- Participate in a forum or workshop (live or online).
- Publish a video on YouTube (link to your website).

Sponsoring and Pro-Bono Work

- Sponsor a local event.
- Sponsor a youth sports team.
- Volunteer your professional servicers pro bono to a well-connected non-profit organization.

Why is pro bono work important and how do you make it win-win?

First, pro bono work is at the core of our values and you are the beneficiary of the good fortune to be talented and capable of having an impact on your world. You have a responsibility to give back and make things better for those not so fortunate.

But second, pro bono service has to work for us as contributors of talent. Our time and skills are assets with monetary values. While we may not benefit directly from our service to an organization, one important benefit should be the broadening of our sphere of influence with people in a position to spread the word about the value and importance of the work we do..

Here is an example of a current project you may find interesting.

The ***Business Survival Project*** is a hybrid business development program with a lead generation component. It has a legitimate pro bono feature with solid social responsibility credentials. By raising awareness of the need for emergency preparedness in the face of growing natural and man-made disasters, the program encourages expanded consultative engagement by professional advisers serving the small-to-medium size business (SMB) market. It invites existing clients and prospective new clients to request valuable, complimentary preparedness information to get the process started.

For more information, see Appendix Five or for a complete description of the Pilot Program, visit the website at http://ProfessionalsMarketingMachine.com/Business-Survival-Project/

WHAT ABOUT ATTENDING CONVENTIONS?

Willie Sutton, the famous robber, was asked, "Why do you rob banks?" Supposedly he answered, "That's where the money is."

Whether or not he really said that, the point is well taken. Use numbers to your advantage. Rather than spend your resources on one or two potential clients a day, get in front of dozens or even hundreds of prospects at a convention or conference.

But don't waste your time at a convention – or at the wrong convention.

Don't just participate as an attendee. Give a speech, teach a breakout session related to your specialty . . . and purposefully network. Visit vendor booths, strike up conversations with salespeople, supervisors and, yes, even maintenance and security staff. Mention a white paper, article or checklist. If they express interest, make a note on the back of your business card and give it to them. And be sure to get one of their cards as well.

(I know, today's conventions keep track of attendance by swiping your registration ID tag. But the people you want to meet and talk with don't walk around carrying an RFID reader. Keeping notes in your handheld device works for YOU, but the person you've met typically goes away with nothing. That's why we like business cards.)

Don't depend on your memory alone. Make or record notes about everyone and your conversation with them. Follow up with an email. (If this doesn't sound familiar, go back and re-read Chapter 3 about referrals and networking.)

Conferences can be a real boon to your marketing efforts, but beware of treating them casually. Preparing your networking plan in advance, doing the research and knowing whom you plan to connect with is really a mini-marketing plan.

We've included a proven **Conference and Convention Planning Guide** in the Appendix. Use this guide to magnify the results you get from the next seminar or conference you attend.

This is the heart of your success in whatever business or specialty you think you're in. Remember, **marketing is your real business**. If you neglect your marketing, the rest is just a hobby!

Caution: You may NOT want to attend conferences put on by your own professional association.

If it's a learning opportunity, great. If there are other participants not in direct competition with you, exchanging information on potential clients can be mutually beneficial.

But unless your peers in your niche are going to refer business to you, it could (and often is) a waste of your time.

Think about it this way, if you're too busy to handle all the business trying to fall in over your transom, which leads are you going to refer to a competitor? Certainly not the best ones . . . assuming you know the difference.

WITH SO MANY POTENTIAL MARKETING ACTIVITIES, WHERE SHOULD I BEGIN?

Focus on the opportunity – and your strengths.

Don't let these lists of marketing activities intimidate you. Skim through and identify a few of the options that look attractive and **that you already are confident about**. Start with them and push your comfort zone once you have some successes under your belt.

Like to meet and greet? Jump to the second and third set of suggestions that involve presenting.

Not so comfortable in front of a big crowd? Focus on the first list, and polish your writing skills. (There are lots of opportunities for re-purposing good material you've already created!)

But **expect to engage in activities from each set**. If meeting people or giving talks scares the living sh*t out of you, join a Toastmasters Group and get over it! There's no room in the professional world for a wallflower. People like dealing with confident winners.

Create a calendar.

Wherever you decide to begin, consider creating a personal "marketing calendar" for the next full year. Start by filling in the dates of major conventions, conferences or meetings – even local half-day seminars – you think might be worthwhile to attend or speak at. Spread them out to give yourself time between dates to prepare and then to follow up with the people you met. (Speaker arrangements are often made a year in advance.)

Each of these activities and major events becomes a marketing project in itself. Take the time to brainstorm everything you'll need to do in advance, everything you'll need to have at the event, what follow-up activities are necessary to get full benefit of your investment. Consider building an "event planning checklist" that you can use over and over again.

And about that last item on the list, sponsoring.

Many local attorneys and accountants seem to like this "hand's free" advertising. Just put up a few dollars and get back to the office. Supporting local young people or a local event may not be a waste of money, but it may be a waste of opportunity if you don't follow the money. Get out there and participate. Show people you really care and you could be surprised at the rewards, personal as well as financial.

HOLD THIS THOUGHT:

You have the choice of spending your resources – time, energy and money – on single targets or you can direct your energies in pursuit of multiple contacts who, in turn, represent several potential contacts of their own. What opportunities do you have to connect with dozens, hundreds or even thousands of individuals with one effort?

Note: We offer a unique lead generation campaign opportunity that is also a public relations campaign built around saving lives and property. It can be conducted on a small or large scale and has measurable results. Check it out in the Appendix under "Emergency Plan Guide Lead Generation Opportunity."

11 - Your Website is the Hub of Your Marketing Plan.

Your website controls your message.

The need for quality, relevant content.

Choosing a flexible platform.

"It's just an electronic brochure . . . What's the big deal?"

"People only go to my website to verify that I'm really who I say I am. They aren't interested in reading a lot of stuff they already know."

You don't really believe that or you wouldn't be reading this book.

Forgive me for slipping into "rant mode" here – I'll be brief.

In the graveyard of failed companies, some of the tombstones would probably read, "The website was a piece of art, but nobody came to see it."

I have a rant on this subject that dates back to the 1980s and it will likely appear on <u>my</u> tombstone!

Warning: Don't let a graphic artist anywhere near your marketing materials until you have your copy platform and some working headlines down on paper.

You have to guide artists in their conceptualizing to make certain the art doesn't overpower (or misrepresent) the copy. That includes your website design as well as your printed brochures, direct mail pieces or anything you expect to market your products and/or services.

Marketing and sales are foreign to many artists' thinking.

Why? The more talented the artist, the more premature creative design can be off somewhere in the land of Oz. Artists just plain think differently than sales people. And that's why we love them. But their vivid imagination and design skills are best utilized **after** you've laid the marketing foundation and the communication parameters.

OK, back to the value and purpose of your website!

Your website is constantly working.

One way to think of your website is like a sticky tarpaper, black hole or whirlpool. It is constantly . . .

1. **Attracting** interested visitors, people searching the web for specific information or being referred from another source;

2. **Qualifying** them as potential (prospective) clients with articles, data, or other structured content;

3. **Categorizing** them according to their particular interests in your products or services and;

4. **Engaging** them with offers of information they can request. By responding to specific offers they are, in effect, segmenting their interest and even qualifying their interests;

5. **Providing** you with the means to communicate with them by leaving their name, email, and in some cases even their address and phone number.

In other words, through the quality and quantity of your excellent content, you keep them engaged long enough to determine their interests and (if appropriate) set up further communications.

At what point do you personally engage with these prospects? That's where your Sales Process (that we outlined in Chapter 7) comes in.

Appropriate and required features for the site.

Finding out the appropriate features for YOUR website will require some homework on your part.

- If we want the website to project "authority" in your field you will have to make sure that the content is consistently high quality.
- You'll need to know what information your prospects regularly search for or, alternatively, what they are searching for this week. (This could be driven by something that appeared in the news or something YOU did, like publish a book or give a talk.)
- You'll want to understand how sophisticated their searches are and what search terms they type into Google or one of the other search engines.
- How willing are your visitors to read to the end of a long article? Using analytics tools you'll learn the optimum length for your articles.
- As time goes on you will also know how much information your visitors are willing to give you in return for a "free" offer. (The more

info you ask for, the less response you'll get.)
- What do you want visitors to do? Request a free offer? Attend a seminar? Call you right now? The call to action will require not only messaging but also the background technology to capture names, send out confirmations, etc.

A true authority website will have a high volume of relevant pages containing the more competitive (and difficult to rank for) keywords and phrases plus an option on every page for the visitor to take another step up the ladder to a relationship.

The importance of including only high quality content cannot be overstated!

We don't really like the phrase "content is king." Not because it's untrue, but we feel that it reduces the power of ideas, facts, revelations and opinions to some sort of commodity or common denominator.

Semantics aside, whatever your field of endeavor, the depth and breadth of the information, data, Illustrations, discoveries, theories and forecasts that make up your content and distinguish your site will attract visitors in ever growing numbers.

But they won't all enter the site the same way.

It's estimated that something like 80-90% or more of visitors to an authoritative site come, not to the home page, but to **specific pages focused on information they are interested in, including "offers" that you may have advertised.** Before we get too deep into some of the necessary mechanics, let's talk about the offers you might make.

Some things in life are free . . . at least sort of free.

You can regularly post survey data or the results of specific research that you can be sure your visitors will want to know about. You want to give away enough of your "intellectual content" to hook your visitors and keep them coming back and back.

Sometimes a little bribery is in order.

Having visitors' emails allows you to send them information on either a regular or irregular schedule. To get people to give you their emails you'll need to offer something in exchange. For some practices, valuable "bribery" content might be a simple checklist; other professional sites may need to offer entire books, high-level research papers, etc. (**Note that when you are asking people to give you their contact info in return for your materials, using the word "free" is inaccurate and could even be considered illegal.**)

How about selling information products?

Now we're opening up the real can of worms. Millions of websites offer information products for sale or earn commissions by referring visitors to other products or services. So why not you?

Well, as a professional you may be expected to be above the fray. On the other hand, professionals selling their own books on their own site can position the sale as an exclusive benefit.

This is a decision you will have to make depending on your particular positioning . . . especially if you want to become known as an authority site. Enough said, you're on your own here.

What is the role of SEO (Search Engine Optimization)? Does it really make a difference?

Yes, it absolutely does, but it continues to be refined over the years to keep pace with changes introduced by the different browsers. Browsers seek to provide an ever faster and better user experience (spelled UX in some circles!) – and you should want to, too. Better user experience makes fans who want to return again and again. And in your case, the authority of the site grows steadily.

Don't mistake this as an encouragement to overuse key words. Your "authority" is ultimately determined by people, not computers. If you are a real thought leader, prove it. Your website is just a platform. Your written materials, opinion pieces, white papers, videos, blog posts and ultimately your book (books) are what will validate your website and keep your readers coming back. On that note, let's move on.

Does your website intrigue, validate or chase prospective clients away?

Assembling all the pieces that make up the whole of your website may seem daunting. And for many it is overwhelming, especially in the beginning when resources are stretched thin. But you can't wait too long to build the site or technology advances will overtake you.

If you already have a website, you may want to skip over the next few paragraphs. But if you're not happy with the one you have, or don't have one at all, take a look.

The solution to a website that will serve for a few years at least is an underlying software platform that makes the components of the website dynamic, flexible and responsive. Among the easiest to use and the most popular is the WordPress platform, which is currently credited with running over 30% of all internet sites. Here are some dramatic WordPress statistics:

- WordPress' 2018 share of the global CMS (Content Management System) market equals near 60% – making it the most popular CMS of them all for the 8th year in a row.
- The New Yorker, Bloomberg Professionals, Sony Music, Disney, TED, Beyonce, BBC America, Variety, The Home Depot, UPS, Zillow, Yelp and IBM all use WordPress.
- WordPress is the fastest growing CMS, with roughly 500+ new sites being built daily in the top 10 million websites on the web (compared to Shopify's and Squarespace's 60-80).

- WordPress powers many of the top 100 websites in the world.
- 17 blog posts are published every second on WordPress sites around the world.
- 37 million global Google searches for "WordPress" are entered every month.

Note: there are two WordPress platforms. The first is WordPress.com. This is NOT the Website CMS described above. WordPress.com is strictly a site for hosting blogs. While it is free, users give up ownership of the content and any list of followers. You want the CMS version, i.e., **WordPress.org**.

WordPress is easy to use . . . and it's FREE.

The WordPress site is free to set up. As noted, you own both the content and any list of visitors that sign up at the site. WordPress is so user friendly that you can do your own entries and updates, but you will have to pay a nominal amount per month for hosting the site.

There are thousands of hosting sites: Bluehost, HostGator and GoDaddy are among the most popular. All things considered, the WordPress platform is an ideal, easy to use startup CMS. As your site grows you can decide if you require a different platform.

Website "themes" set the graphic interface and basic layout for the site. Once again, there is a big selection of themes out there. Some are free themes; others cost a one-time or recurring fee. In any case, you want a theme (perhaps specific to your industry?) from a company that maintains and updates regularly.

All this basic information about websites is not meant to encourage you to think you can build your own site – though you may be tempted! Rather, it is designed to show that websites are not hard to come by. But let a professional website designer build the site while you build your professional practice. Just be sure you provide them with the marketing and sales strategy to keep them headed in the right direction.

And now to finish this rambling diatribe, let's deal with the real elephant in the room!

HOLD THIS THOUGHT:

By publishing a website you become a publisher. The "content" you publish and how you promote your site opens the door to ever widening audiences. It begins to give you more than a local platform. You have the opportunity to reach regional, national and even international audiences. From this base you can conduct webinars, podcasts, e-newsletter and more. Something to think about!

12 - The Role of Publishing in Establishing Your "Authority"

Writing skills are an advantage, not a requirement.

All your writings become your body of work.

Are you ready to write your book?

Let's see if we can make a huge point here and do it as painlessly as possible.

Maybe English isn't your native language. Or, creative as you are, you may have found ways to goof off during English class (which might even have been taught by a phys. ed. major, as mine was). Maybe you experienced trauma at an early age when an English teacher admonished you for poor grammar. Perhaps you had a poem or love note rejected publicly by someone you had a crush on. Maybe you actually submitted a manuscript to a publisher, only to receive a rejection letter.

Well so what? You aren't alone.

Both Hemingway and J.K. Rowling got rejection letters. Harry Potter was rejected by 12 different editors before it went on to become the repeat blockbuster we all know. Obviously, being rejected doesn't mean you should fade away into obscurity. These authors got their revenge and you can too.

Whatever your challenges, your professional status is at risk if you can't master the written word.

REST EASY. HELP IS EVERYWHERE FOR YOU.

In the midst of today's business whirlwind, we are experiencing college seniors unable to write a coherent resume. Our President, arguably the most important and powerful person in the world, struggles to make his point with a fifth grade vocabulary. Sometimes it seems it's a miracle that anything in business gets done at all!

But the saving grace for you and me is that, while the demand is high, the standards are so low for the written word that we don't have to be a Hemingway or a J.K. Rowling to stand out.

Indeed, as professionals in today's world we only have to be able to clearly convey our ideas, our observations, recommendations and rational conclusions to succeed in a professional capacity.

Fortunately we have the option taken by politicians and executives everywhere to rely on **speechwriters and ghostwriters** to polish the expression of our ideas.

Legions of people work for a fraction of your hourly rate as competent **editors, grammarians and proofreaders.** They are eminently hirable to provide guidance to clean up and strengthen speeches, public letters and other writings.

You're not comfortable writing? How about talking? **Speech recognition products** like Dragon Naturally Speaking "learn" your voice patterns and type your words into the computer as if you were writing them yourself.

If poor acoustics make it difficult for the software to discern between words and competing conversations, **transcription services** provided by real people can turn your talks, comments on interviews or panel discussions into accurate printed documents.

Are these options perfect? No, but they are tools for you to use to get your opinions, your wisdom and your celebrity into print.

Opinion papers, articles white papers and commentaries are important milestones. But it's your book that will get you over the finish line.

The important people and major corporations you are seeking as clients have their own reputation and credibility to protect. They will do their due diligence on your background, values and reputation. Your book becomes a major factor in their justification for working with you.

Getting a book published is simply one of the most important things you can do for your credibility. If you have original ideas, and the ability to convey them either verbally or in writing, you are in a position to light a fuse under your career.

Just as the internet unlocked the world of advertising and selling, the advent of digital publishing and print-on-demand have put being a "published author" within reach of far more people.

You should be one of them. You can become one of them.

Throughout this book we've talked about the value of being a **recognized expert** when it comes to boosting referrals, attracting the kinds of clients you want, and pre-selling them.

Your book becomes the very best tool at each step!

It fulfills a wide range of the consultants' needs. Your book can highlight success stories, describe your services and the challenges you take on as well as provide a roadmap of how you systematically tackle and solve client problems.

We've developed a professional's **book-writing startup kit** and are looking for input as we develop a full-fledged course. (See more about it in the Appendix.) When you're ready, request it!

And one last thought. If you feel this book has given you some new ideas or added confidence in your ability to build your practice, drop Virginia or me a note and look for our next book that will address your specific industry or specialty. And we always appreciate honest reviews at Amazon.

Thank you for taking the time to read our book.

Joseph Krueger & Virginia Nicols

HOLD THIS THOUGHT:

A common response from people who have written and published their own book about their business is that it has been life changing and exploded their business horizons. (And that includes some who used a ghost writer!) Is there a book in your future?

Appendices

A few of the topics in this book stimulate more questions than we wanted to include in the body. The Appendices offer more detail.

1 – The Workbook – a Companion to The Marketing Machine® for Professional Services

2 -- Conferences and Conventions: Seven Questions to Ask Before You Invest in Your Next One

3 – The Direct Mail Process – an Overview of the Steps and Their Lingo

4 – Write Your Book! – Next Steps for Becoming an Author – and an Authority

5—A Unique Lead-Generation Program for Professionals

Other areas we couldn't cover in depth: networking, strategic alliances, public speaking, radio & TV appearances, detailed website execution, white papers, teaching, and more. Some of these subjects are covered in more detail on our specific industry websites as well as in additional publications.

1 - THE MARKETING MACHINE® FOR PROFESSIONAL SERVICES – THE WORKBOOK

Yes, we've already mentioned THE WORKBOOK. We feel it is essential to getting your marketing programs to actually take shape.

Reading about how to solve marketing challenges is one way to get new ideas for your practice. But we believe that reading alone may not be enough to help you work on **the why and how** of your professional life!

THE WORKBOOK is meant to engage you in another and deeper level of discovery. It's laid out as a series of questions roughly paralleling the content of this book. But then, there is **space for you to write your answers** – or doodle, cross out, highlight, whatever you do when you are really participating in the exercise!

We are big believers in marrying the kinetic energy of your physical handwriting with the potential energy of your mind.

Accordingly, THE WORKBOOK is a full-sized, 8 ½ x 11 paperback. You can find out more at our website http://ProfessionalsMarketingMachine.com

2-Conferences and Conventions: Seven Questions to Ask Before You Invest in Your Next One

You see an announcement about an upcoming conference or convention.

It's going to be held in a city that's always been on your "bucket list." The marketing copy is full of references to an "intimate setting" with "senior corporate peers," and "return on investment." It's labeled **"The one conference you don't want to miss!"**

There's even an announcement that one of the exhibitors will be featuring a "virtual reality" demonstration.

You are torn! It sounds great, and if it's truly the one you don't want to miss, then you don't want to miss it!

On the other hand, you're thinking: "But this is going to cost me at least a couple thousand dollars. And I'll be out of the office for a full week. How can I justify that when I'm just starting a new marketing effort?"

Our answer is simple.

Admittedly, trade shows and conventions can be costly. But they bring people and ideas together and create **opportunities that are simply not available otherwise**.

The purpose of this report is to identify those opportunities and how to take full advantage of them.

In many cases, it's simply a question of **avoiding a misstep**.

This report's seven key questions will give you a proven path to follow. It's an easy read and full of suggestions you'll be able to apply immediately. (Virginia adds, "You can also use this report to guide and evaluate the effectiveness of employees you send to conferences.")

So jump in – and enjoy it!

INTRODUCTION – THE CONFERENCE INVESTMENT
It's relatively easy to measure the financial cost of attending a convention. I'm

sure you've added up the registration fee, the bill for travel and accommodations, costs for a booth (if you are participating as an exhibitor) and the cost of your and any staff time.

But as the owner of a small business, particularly if you are starting on a new marketing initiative, attending a convention represents a lot bigger investment than hard dollars!

- It **pulls you away** from your personal marketing plan.
- It can **halt the momentum** of your on-going marketing efforts.
- It can **interrupt the work** of other people in your organization.

So if you make the convention choices, you stand to lose a lot more than just money!

We're not recommending that you avoid conventions or trade shows all together. We are convinced that they offer opportunities you can't get elsewhere.

The trick is to set yourself up to take full advantage of them!

Spend some time with the seven questions. Your answers will give you the confidence that you won't be wasting the investment!

And our guarantee: If you aren't sure about some of your answers the first time through, this report has **enough suggestions in every section to get you right back on track!**

QUESTION ONE – HAVE YOU PICKED THE RIGHT SHOW?
Going to the wrong conference or convention is like going on a bad date. You have high expectations but come away discouraged and poorer.

So your first goal is to identify which conventions to attend – and why.

For the owner of a new business, this depends on whether you are staying in your "old" industry, where you already have contacts, or expanding your horizons.

If you are established in your industry, but in the start-up phase of a new marketing effort, a convention may be the very best way for you to quickly introduce yourself in your new role – and to get in touch with some needed business resources.

As a known commodity, you may also find the opportunity to be **a speaker at the convention.** (In this case, be sure to contact convention planners early in the planning schedule – as much as a year in advance, certainly within 6 months. And it should go without saying that you need to offer up some sort of "hot topic" or "trend" on which to speak.)

Being a convention speaker offers powerful marketing advantages:

- You control how your company will be branded.
- Your name and company will be promoted by the conference sponsor for months in advance.

- Your presentation may be posted or linked to for weeks or months afterwards.
- You may be featured in real time as part of a virtual conference.
- You have opportunities for self-generated publicity: news releases, articles and white papers – valuable collateral for continuing sales use beyond the show.
- You may be approached for an interview by a conference sponsor, another attendee or the local media, with footage showing up on *YouTube* or on the organization's website.

If you're heading in a new professional direction, though, setting yourself up as an "expert" at a national convention can be risky! People who already know you as a leader in one field could be confused at seeing you wearing a different hat. And the true experts in your new field will probably recognize your inexperience.

So, you may wish to get the benefit of more **basic training** before you plunge into the ranks at a national convention. Top quality basic training may best be found at regional or local conferences or trade shows – and at considerably less cost.

Your choice of which conventions to attend must take all these aspects into consideration. Pick the right ones and you're off to a good start!

P.S. **Tie-breakers**. Naturally, you may prefer one show over another because of add-on vacation options, or because it has a "green" or charitable commitment. If these are important, be sure to add them to your decision-making process.

QUESTION TWO – HAVE YOU SET SPECIFIC GOALS FOR THIS SHOW?
Sure, you are hoping to "make some new connections" or maybe even make sales.

Those are valid goals. But . . . why not give yourself a much better chance of getting real results by setting **a number of**

personal goals as well as business goals? Write them down! For example:

- Renew acquaintances with old friends.
- Connect with key industry suppliers.
- Identify major competitors in the field, and find out what they are doing.
- Put out feelers for a new employee or partner.
- See the latest technology, recognize the latest trends.
- Set up off-site meetings with key prospects or contacts.
- Meet three other business owners in your industry to investigate starting a peer-to-peer coaching group.
- Make contacts that will lead to speaking engagements over the next 12 months.

Which of your goals belong to which session at the show?

The more specific you are as you outline your goals, the more opportunities you'll discover for reaching them. If you don't take the time to set your goals in advance, you may find yourself mingling with the wrong people and missing opportunities with the right people.

Keep track of how you're doing as the show goes on. Without goals, and without managing them, you may find yourself on the last day having spent the time and money with little or nothing to show for it.

QUESTION THREE – WHO DO YOU WANT TO CONNECT WITH?
Who do you want to meet at this upcoming convention? Do you plan to meet different people at the next one? Each show may have a different target audience.

As part of your personal networking plan, you may already have identified people you want to meet. The question: Will they be at this convention?

Contact them directly to find out!

In most cases the registration materials will get you started on your list of who to connect with. Your list should probably start with the person who's the "big name" draw!

You can also use recent editions of professional or trade publications to identify other interesting or important people who will likely be present: trainers, association officials, suppliers or exhibitors, members of the press, colleagues and friends.

<u>Build a database</u> of your contact list, with titles, addresses and reasons why you want to meet. Make sure you have pertinent information on your contacts' accomplishments and their affiliations for ready reference.

<u>Schedule your activities</u>. Use the registration materials to study the various events that will be taking place. Don't skip over breakfasts, cocktail parties or hospitality suites, often the best place to solidify relationships or uncover new opportunities.

Mark sessions you need to attend to meet specific people or educational goals.

Identify the sessions being led by people on your contacts list. Some people may be at the meeting only on the day of their own presentation.

List the names of the specific speakers or exhibitors you want to speak to during each exhibit period. Keep in mind that the people you connect with may not be potential clients, but can become powerful sources of referral.

Contact in advance all the people you want to meet at the convention, and begin to set appointments. **Start with the key-note speaker, who is likely to be the hardest to schedule.** Consider breakfast meetings, lunch, or other appointments. Perhaps you can meet at the airport or even fly together.

Have an agenda for each individual meeting. Be sure you are ready to explain exactly why you'd like to meet and how long your meeting should last. Have a call-to-action ready, to make sure you move to the next step after the convention is over. Everyone at the event will be pressed for time, and will appreciate your attention to detail.

<u>Check with clients or prospects</u> that might be at the seminar. If they don't plan to go, find out the main things they are interested in, add those goals to your list, and make plans to meet with these people and fill them in when you're back in town.

<u>Keep track in real time</u>. Event-management software may allow you to manage your entire schedule via your phone or tablet.

QUESTION FOUR – DO YOU HAVE A CHEAT SHEET FOR EACH SESSION?
In advance, develop an evaluation sheet for each session and activity you plan to attend. It should contain these sections:

- Name of session
- Time, place
- Leader or contact person
- Questions to get answered

- Actions you want to take

Here's a quick example in the form of an actual sheet of paper. You can turn it into a digital form, of course, if you prefer.

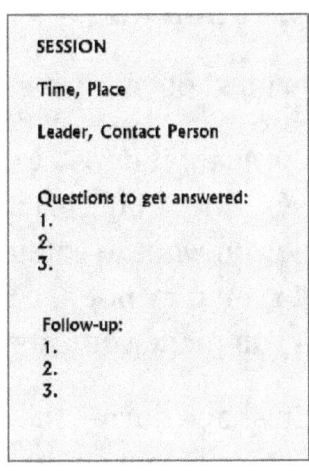

Use your evaluation sheet to record ideas during a session or immediately after a meeting. Write them or dictate.

Nowadays it's common to find attendees with their laptops or tablets on the table, taking notes during the presentation. (And checking their email, browsing Instagram images, etc.!)

You can also tape sessions – it it's allowed.

QUESTION FIVE – ARE YOU PRIMED FOR NETWORKING?

When you aren't at a pre-arranged meeting, take advantage of networking opportunities. **Profitable networking takes preparation and energy!**

To make the most of your time..

- Review again the roster of attendees. Check off the names of people you want to connect with, people you may not have noted when you made your first schedule.

- Stay in shape during the convention: exercise, get enough sleep, eat and drink sensibly. If you allow yourself to become fatigued, you will project a poor image to people who only have the opportunity to see you this way.

- Wear comfortable clothes and shoes and avoid dragging around heavy briefcases or bags. (If you don't have a room where you can stash materials, check items with the bell captain or prevail upon an exhibitor friend to borrow space beneath an exhibit table.)

- Bring at least 100 business cards. (Yes, you may have heard that business cards are passé. Not so at conventions!) But don't pass out a single one to an individual without first making a note on the back – your cell phone number, the topic you were discussing, a possible next step. Make notes on the cards you receive, too. Otherwise the importance or context of your contact may be lost. Be prepared to capture other people's contact information via smart phone technology.

- Be systematic about covering exhibits, realizing you probably can't visit them all. Most registration materials include a map of the exhibit area. Use a colored pen to plan your route from targeted booth to booth – a different color for each exhibit period. Again, convention management software may make this easier. However you do it, do it!

- If you need to, practice your "two-sentence introduction" - a brief description of what you do and how it relates to your contact's interests. In some cases, you may need to include something about how that person used to know you, and what you are doing now and how that might benefit them. Practice a sentence that suggests what the other person can do for you, too. While we're not generally fans of "elevator speeches," it's true that at a convention you have a very short time to make the connection, so be prepared.

- Meet as many new people as you comfortably can. Make it a policy to seek out new faces at every opportunity. Don't hang out with "the gang" at hospitality suites – unless getting back in touch with those "gang members" is one of the goals on your list!

- Use social media to announce your presence to other people at the meeting, and to folks at home. Send tweets. Send a blog post. Tape a quick video and post it on your website. Be sure you have all the equipment and/or resources you need to communicate this way! (Don't forget passwords, extra batteries, connector cables, etc.)

QUESTION SIX – WHAT'S YOUR PLAN FOR FOLLOWING UP?

Follow-up activities provide a wealth of marketing opportunities. They should be your first priority since the longer you wait, the more you forget. Here are a few ideas..

- Send personal thank-you notes, or make phone calls, to new acquaintances. Plan a strategy for future communications.

- Mail or e-mail information to people to whom you promised it, delivered with a personal message and a clear call to action for the next step in your relationship.

- File your materials, including samples from the exhibits, so you'll be able to use them as resources. In many cases, you will receive materials only AFTER the convention has ended, and then, via email. (Too many people simply throw away those expensive printed brochures they pick up at the exhibits, rather than lug them home again!)

- Develop and present a talk about the convention. If you have employees, give it to them. If you belong to a local business networking group, perhaps it would be appropriate for them. Turn it into SlideShare and post on LinkedIn and on your own website. This single step will position you and brand your business as a leader.

- Send a postcard, e-mail or tweet from the convention site to important clients. And make a follow-up call or send a follow-up message with recommendations for action.

- Put together a seminar for prospects, referral sources or clients on the latest developments in the industry. (You may want to make preliminary arrangements and send out invitations even before the convention takes place.) Make recommendations for action.

- Write an article outlining new information for release in the local press. Make sure readers know how to get in touch with you.

- Write an article for your website. Suggest resources, invite questions. Be the expert.

- Ask one of the convention speakers to speak to your clients or to your local industry association. Interview the speaker for a podcast that you can share. Develop him or her into a referral source.

QUESTION SEVEN – HOW DO YOU MEASURE VALUE?

Planning and managing your seminar and convention attendance will open the door to many new marketing opportunities like those listed above. Keep track of them, and of their results.

It may take only **one good idea** to justify the cost of the convention many times over.

Perhaps more importantly, attending a convention can give you vital feedback on where you and your company stand with regard to the competition and the standards within your industry. This marketing intelligence might otherwise be unavailable or obtainable only at great cost. Make sure you document your findings and incorporate them into your long-range business planning.

Measuring Return on Investment can be a comprehensive exercise. At the very least, **complete a simple evaluation** – like the one-page "Appraisal" we've included below.

The most important question is the one at the very bottom of the form!

Convention Appraisal
Name and Date of Show

Why this particular show?

Goals for this show – personal and business

Key people to contact

Key sessions/activities to schedule

Follow-up marketing activities (also for people who did NOT attend

Evaluation positives

Evaluation negatives

Go again next year? YES NO

Copyright 2017 The Marketing Machine®. All rights reserved

FINAL THOUGHTS

If you are worried about the registration cost of a conference either it's not worth going to or you're undervaluing your time.

Most good seminars or conventions are worth ten times as much as they cost, but you'll only get that return if you prepare for each one and manage the investment of your time.

We hope this special report will give you the encouragement and the guidance you need to be sure that next conference is the right one.

3-The Direct Mail Process

We find that there's a lot of confusion about how direct mail works as a marketing tool. Earlier we talked about how the list, offer and creative interact. And in Chapter 9 we slipped in reference to our **bonus infographic** for B2B marketers.

On the next page we're providing an overview of how the entire campaign comes together.

This is just an overview, not the actual step-by-step process you'll actually be following. Still, it gives you an idea of how systematic everything has to be. The little chart also includes some of the "lingo" of the trade.

When lists are easy to acquire, production is straightforward and scheduling goes without a hitch, days can be cut from the process. In every case, solid planning at the beginning of the campaign helps set the stage for success.

Planning (weeks 1-2)
Consult / Define / Background / Market / Logistics / Plan

Creative (weeks 3-4)
Concepts / Final Art / Production / Media / Final Copy & Design

Production (weeks 5-6)
Graphics / Proofing / List Merge-Purge / Final Approval / Print & Bind

Execution (weeks 7-8)
Address / Assemble / Insert / Drop

Tracking (week 9 --)
Response / Conversions / Projections / Revisions

4-WRITE YOUR BOOK!

If you're seriously considering becoming an author; if you want the authority (and maybe even the bragging rights!) that a published book can bestow, there are well-established guidelines to make sure you get that book written!

We have completed a **Book-Writing Start-Up Kit** for business authors. Here are some of the questions in the Kit that you can start considering right now. You'll quickly see how they would help guide the development of your book:

- Do you know who your audience will be? Will they actually be enthusiastic about your material?
- Have you been around long enough to know these readers' problems and to have credible solutions for them?
- Do you have stories from your own experience to help get your message across?
- Do you have specific processes you follow in your services to clients?

- Are there gaps in prospective clients' knowledge that make them hesitant to engage your services?
- Have you kept up with recent developments and can you comment on changes in the industry?
- Have you built relationships with other leaders in your industry or niche, people who will be willing to help spread the word about your book?

These questions are part of the Start-Up Kit. Our next step is to finalize a number of decisions about the full course, which will be ready soon. We invite you to **request the Book-Writing Start-up Kit** so you'll be on our list when the course rolls out. Just send a message to my website: Http://JosephKrueger.com/contact/

5- *Business Survival Project*: A Lead Generation Program Uniquely Suited for Professional Services Firms

The **Business Survival Project** is a hybrid Business Development Program with a Lead Generation Component and a legitimate pro bono aspect with solid social responsibility credentials.

It is a three-part program that starts with a unique business development concept – offering new consulting opportunities with client businesses.

Expands Your Business Advisory Credentials

As a professional adviser, you offer to work with your existing clients on a new aspect of their business – to help build a plan for their business survival. The plan is outlined in a step-by-step process in ***Emergency Preparedness for Small Business***, a simple book that you make available to clients at no cost. Using its fifty-page companion Workbook plus materials we provide as part of the project, creating a plan for the business is surprisingly easy – and it also is likely to uncover opportunities to streamline their business operations.

Whether or not your client decides to move ahead with full planning, introducing the project gives you an opportunity to expand your relationship. You will not only add to the client's profitability to your firm, but also demonstrate the value of your consulting services. Other new opportunities may also open as a result.

What is my next step?

Satisfy yourself that this makes sense for your business as well as your clients. The best way to do this is to go to Amazon.com and purchase one or more sets of the book *Emergency Preparedness for Small Business* and the companion Workbook. Discuss the opportunity internally and even with members of your business community.

Then, if you want to learn more, go to http://ProfessionalsMarketingMachine.com/Business-Survival-Project/ and request an Application package. It has questions about the number of clients you wish to include in the Pilot Program, a description of your marketing area by zip code/s (We want to minimize conflicts between two or more competing firms.) and the number of "leads" or inquiries you are comfortable handling per week and total over a 90-day period.

If your situation fits the parameters of the test program, we will contact you to discuss. And if appropriate, provide you with an outline of costs and time frame.

Some Final Words and a Couple of Offers from the Authors

Joe Krueger and Virginia Nicols

If you haven't figured it out by now, we have been in the marketing and publishing business for quite a while. When you combine all our experience, it totals to over 50 years!

It's treated us well – and we still like it and write every day!

We are actively looking for projects where we can bring our collective body of marketing experience to bear, whether it's helping a sole practitioner break through to a new level of success, or whether it's helping a whole neighborhood organize itself to prepare for disasters. (You'll see some of our published works on emergency preparedness on Amazon, too.)

One thing we've learned is that people want information and help not necessarily when they need it, but when they want it! To that end, we try to make some training materials available for whenever the impulse hits.

At our website https://TheMarketingMachineGroup.com you'll find a collection of free articles and courses for sale. Since you've already read this book you may want to take a look at these courses, in particular:

- Be a Power Presenter!
- Website – The Hub of Your Marketing Plan
- Better eMail Copy
- Strategic Marketing Plan for Professionals
- Professional Networking Guide

You can download these marketing materials anytime, day or night. Each course is easy to read, in step-by-step format, and comes with a workbook.

Finally, as we described in the Appendix, we are particularly eager to help people who are ready to take the next step toward publishing their authority book. Our book-writing course will be formally introduced in 2019.

Part of our course will be personal consulting to get you off to a solid start. Naturally, we'll only be offering consulting to a limited number of people, so if you think you'll be interested, **request the Book-Writing Start-Up Kit now** to get to the top of the list. We look forward to hearing from you!

Joe
http://JosephKrueger.com/contact

Virginia
http://VirginiaNicols.com/contact

www.ingramcontent.com/pod-product-compliance
Lightning Source LLC
Chambersburg PA
CBHW052313220526
45472CB00001B/95